TRUTH
TRUT

Exposing the Myth of Evolution

BE TOLD

KYLE BUTT
AND ERIC LYONS

Truth Be Told: Exposing the Myth of Evolution

by Kyle Butt and Eric Lyons

First Edition © 2005
Second Edition © 2009

Apologetics Press

Printed in China

Layout and Design by Charles McCown, Jim Estabrook, and Moisés Pinedo

Consulting and writing assistance:
Wayne Jackson, M.A.
Dave Miller, Ph.D.
Brad Harrub, Ph.D.
Bert Thompson, Ph.D.
Apologetics Press interns

Apologetics Press, Inc.
230 Landmark Drive
Montgomery, Alabama 36117
U.S.A.

Dedication

To our daughters: Anna Claire Butt and Shelby Ruth Lyons—whose sweet dispositions have shown us the fact that children truly are a reward from our heavenly Father (Psalm 127:3).

Library of Congress Cataloging-in-Publication

Kyle Butt (1976 -) and Eric Lyons (1975 -)

Truth Be Told: Exposing the Myth of Evolution

Includes subject index.

ISBN 978-0-932859-84-6

1. Creation. 2. Science and Religion. I. Title

213—dc22   2005926365

TABLE OF CONTENTS

Chapter 7—Dinosaurs and Man.........................113

Chapter 8—Evolution is not a Proven Fact.........135

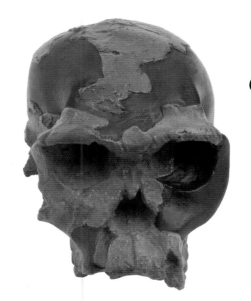

CHAPTER-1
THE ORIGIN OF THE UNIVERSE

How did this huge, marvelous Universe get here? In many of the science textbooks that you read, you will be taught that the Universe started from the Big Bang. According to this idea, the Universe was packed into a very dense ball of matter that was about as big as a period at the end of a sentence. This little ball of matter supposedly exploded about 14 billion years ago. The explosion, which is called the Big Bang, is said to have sent matter and space expanding as the Universe was formed. The clumps of matter that were sent shooting through space started to form orbiting galaxies and planets. The Big Bang theory is the theory most science books are teaching today to explain the origin of the Universe.

Because the Big Bang theory is about an explosion that supposedly took place in the distant past, and because Big Bangs are not happening today, evolutionists can no more "test" the Big Bang and how life supposedly evolved from non-life than creationists can scientifically test God and Creation. Just as supernatural six-day creations are not taking place today for us to observe, there are no big bangs to examine and experiment on. So really, neither creationists nor evolutionists can use the scientific method to prove that their ideas about where we came from are correct.

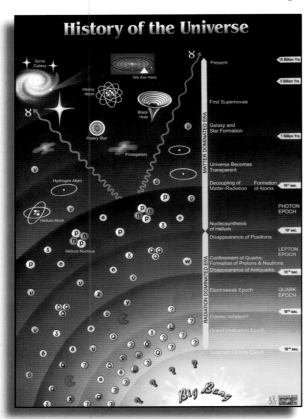

The above chart illustrates the evolutionary view of the origin of the Universe from the Big Bang until the present.

...evolutionists can no more "test" the Big Bang...than creationists can test God....

But, are there things we can **know** about the world today that point to either evolution or Creation being true? Yes, there are. Some of the best scientific facts to consult when wanting to know whether we were created by a supernatural Creator, or whether we evolved by chance over millions of years, are the laws of nature. A scientific law is a principle in nature that is true in every observable case. Whether the measurements come from the sunny islands of Hawaii or the ice-covered tundra of the Arctic, a scientific law is the same for all places. But one thing we must remember about scientific laws is that scientists **do not make the laws, they only observe them and label them**. Isaac Newton's first law of motion, which states that every object in a state of uniform motion tends to stay in that state of motion unless an outside force is applied to it, was a law of nature before Isaac Newton ever named it. Also, scientific laws occur regardless of whether we humans like them or not. If you are standing by a tall building and someone drops a baseball from the top, the scientific law of gravity immediately becomes something to think about—like it or not.

Also, we need to understand the difference between a scientific law and a theory. While a law is something that is observable in every known case, a theory is something that someone **thinks** might have happened in the past or might happen in the future. Over the years, many false theories have been thrown out because they did not agree with the scientific laws of nature. If a theory goes against scientific laws of nature, then the theory is not correct and must be discarded.

Sir Isaac Newton

THE LAW OF CAUSE AND EFFECT

The first problem with the Big Bang theory is that it goes against the Law of Cause and Effect that we see in the Universe. So far as scientific knowledge goes, natural laws have no exceptions. This certainly is true of the Law of Cause and Effect, which is the most universal and most certain of all laws. Simply put, the Law of Cause and Effect states that every **material** effect must have an **adequate** cause that happens before the effect.

Material effects without adequate causes do not exist. Also, causes never occur after the effect. It is meaningless to speak of a cause following an effect, or an effect coming before a cause. In addition, the effect never is greater than the cause. That is why scientists say that every material effect must have an **adequate** cause. The entire river did not turn muddy because a frog jumped into it; neither did the book fall from the table because a gnat landed on it. These are not adequate causes. They are not big enough to produce the effect. As we start to look at the size of the Universe, we will quickly see that a tiny ball of matter is not an adequate cause.

Have you ever gone outside on a clear summer evening and looked up into the night sky? Isn't it a beautiful sight—with all the shining, twinkling stars? Scientists tell us that we can see about 3,000 stars just by using our eyes. But if we use a simple telescope, we can see over 100,000 stars! Can you imagine how big this Universe must be in order to hold that many stars?

Our Universe, however, has many more stars than that. Astronomers (scientists who study planets, stars, and other things in space) suggest that our Universe has over 25 sextillion stars in it (that's the number 25 followed by 21 zeros!). They also say it contains over one billion galaxies, each of which has an estimated 100 billion individual stars.

In fact, the Universe is so large that scientists had to develop a rather unusual way to measure it. For example, when you take a trip in a car or on a plane, you may ask your father or mother how far it is to your destination, and how long it will take to get there. They might answer, "Well, it's 375 miles away, and it will take us about 6 hours to get there."

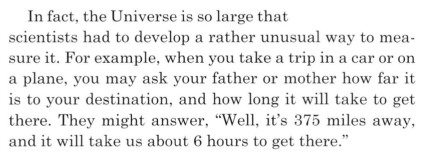

But our Universe is so big that scientists measure it by how long it takes light to go from one spot to another. Light moves so fast that it can go approximately 186,000 miles **in one second**! That means in a year, light can go almost **six trillion miles**. Astronomers call this a "light-year" because it represents the distance that light travels in one year.

The diameter of the Milky Way Galaxy (in which our solar system and the Earth are located) is 100,000 light-years across. That means it is so big that even if you could travel at the speed of light, it still would take 100,000 years just to go across our own galaxy (you would go about **587 quadrillion miles**, and you still would have been in only a single galaxy). If somehow you were able to go from one end of the Universe to the other, astronomers believe it would take you 20 billion years—even traveling at the speed of light! What a marvelous Universe this is in which we live!

The Big Bang could not have caused this huge Universe. Scientists have never seen any type of matter that could be so dense, and then explode from a tiny ball into a Universe like ours. The theory of the Big Bang goes against the scientific Law of Cause and Effect.

THE BIBLE SPEAKS ABOUT THE CAUSE

So, how did the Universe get here? The Bible certainly is not silent about what caused the Universe. In the very first verse of the first chapter of the first book, it says: "In the beginning **God** created the heavens and the Earth." Acts 17:24 records: "**God**, who made the world and everything in it...He is Lord of heaven

Extra Evidence

➤ Even if the Big Bang did occur, which it did not, an explanation would still have to be given for the origin of the tiny ball of matter that supposedly exploded. From nothing, comes nothing.

and earth." Exodus 20:11 notes: "For in six days the **Lord** made the heavens and the earth, the sea, and all that is in them."

God is undoubtedly an adequate cause, since He is all-powerful. In Genesis 17:1, God told Abraham, "I am **Almighty** God."

He existed before this material world, fulfilling the criterion that the cause must come before the effect. The psalmist wrote: "Before the mountains were brought forth, or ever You had formed the earth and the world, even from everlasting to everlasting, You are God" (Psalm 90:2). Only God fits the criterion of an adequate cause that came before the Universe.

WHY DOES GOD NOT HAVE A CAUSE?

Hold on just a minute! If we say that every material effect must have a cause, and we state that only God could have caused the Universe, then the obvious question is: "What caused God?" Doesn't the Law of Cause and Effect apply to God, too?

There is a single word in the Law of Cause and Effect that helps provide the answer to this question— the word **material**. Every **material** effect must have a cause that existed before it. Scientists formulated the Law of Cause and Effect based upon what they have observed while studying this Universe, which is made out of matter. No science experiment in the world can be performed on God, because He is an eternal spirit, not matter (John 4:24). Science is far from learning everything about this material world, and it is even farther from understanding the eternal nature of God. Ultimately, there had to be a first Cause, and God was (and is) the only One suitable for the job.

THE FIRST LAW OF THERMODYNAMICS

Imagine going outside on a snowy day, playing in the cold, wet snow for an hour or two, and going inside to warm up in front of a nice fire. The wood that is burning in the fireplace pops every now and then, and the heat from the fire warms you up and dries off your clothes. If you watch the fire long enough, the wood will burn up and more will be needed to keep the fire going. Have you ever wondered where the wood goes? Does it go out of existence? Is it changed into something else? What happens to the wood?

In thinking about these questions, you have just turned into a physical scientist—one who studies the physical Universe. Now, let's see if we can answer some of those questions about the wood. If you were able to put that fire in a closed box and weigh it before the wood burned, and then weigh the box after the wood

Experiment

You will need a lightweight metal pan, accurate scales, paper, and a match. **Kids, do not try this without adult supervision.**

1. Tear the paper and put it in the pan.

2. Weigh the paper with the pan. Write down the weight.

3. Remove pan with paper from scales and light the paper with the match.

4. Once the flames have completely gone out, weigh the pan with the ashes. How does this weight compare to that of step 2?

burned, you would see that it weighed the same both times. Even though the wood disappeared, it still exists, just in another form. The wood is changed into heat energy, which you can feel on your legs and hands, and certain gases that go into the atmosphere in the smoke that is released by burning. The energy in the wood is changed, but it still exists and none of it is lost.

This little experiment helps us understand one of the most basic laws in nature. It is called the First Law of Thermodynamics. The word thermodynamics comes from two Greek words: *therme* meaning "heat," and *dunamis* meaning "force" or "power." The First Law of Thermodynamics describes the "power" or "energy" contained in heat and its movement to other forms of energy. It says that matter and energy cannot be created or destroyed in nature. Even though wood can burn, the energy is not lost, it simply changes form.

The First Law of Thermodynamics is quite a problem for those who believe in evolution. Here is why. If there is no natural process that can create matter or energy, then how did the material Universe get here in the first place? The evolutionist does not have an answer to this problem. But those who believe in Creation do. If God is supernatural (which means He is above and beyond nature), then He could create matter and energy out of nothing. Belief in God is the only idea that fits with the First Law of Thermodynamics.

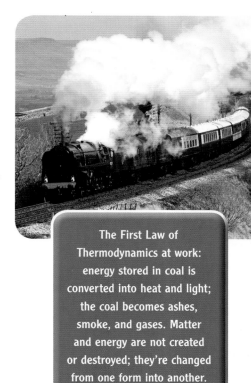

The First Law of Thermodynamics at work: energy stored in coal is converted into heat and light; the coal becomes ashes, smoke, and gases. Matter and energy are not created or destroyed; they're changed from one form into another.

	What did we start with?	What happened?	What did we end up with?
Experiment	paper lit by match	paper burned in air	ashes, light, gases, heat, smoke
Big Bang	"stuff"	Universe expanded	energy & matter make galaxies, stars, planets
Creation	God	miracle of creation	"the heavens and the earth" (Genesis 1:1)

THE SECOND LAW OF THERMODYNAMICS

You probably are old enough to know how to ride a bike. In fact, many of you reading this book probably have your own bicycle. Imagine getting a shiny new, beautiful bicycle for your birthday. The tires are in perfect condition and the paint is spotless without any scratches or chips. What happens to your shiny new bike after you have been riding it for a year? Does the paint look as nice after a year or two as it did when you first bought it? What about the tires, do they stay in perfect condition with great tread? Of course they do not. Your shiny new bike starts getting older and wearing down the minute you begin to ride it.

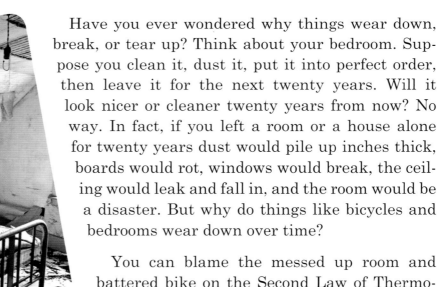

Have you ever wondered why things wear down, break, or tear up? Think about your bedroom. Suppose you clean it, dust it, put it into perfect order, then leave it for the next twenty years. Will it look nicer or cleaner twenty years from now? No way. In fact, if you left a room or a house alone for twenty years dust would pile up inches thick, boards would rot, windows would break, the ceiling would leak and fall in, and the room would be a disaster. But why do things like bicycles and bedrooms wear down over time?

You can blame the messed up room and battered bike on the Second Law of Thermodynamics. Remember, we said the First Law of Thermodynamics says that matter and energy are neither created nor destroyed in nature. They can change forms, but the total amount of energy stays the same. But the Second Law of Thermodynamics says that when matter and energy do change form, they become less usable. Basically, the Second Law says things get more disorderly. Let's see how this works.

Remember the wood in the fireplace. Energy was stored in the wood. When the wood was burned, energy was released as heat and gas. But that heat energy went out into the room and spread out so much that it was no longer useful for heating the house. When the energy in the wood changed into heat energy, it became less usable.

Throughout the entire Universe, the Second Law of Thermodynamics is making energy less usable. Stars are burning out, machines are wearing down, pavement on roads is chipping away, animals and plants die and decay. This law causes every physical thing to break down, wear out, and decay.

This Second Law is also a serious problem for those who believe in evolution. According to evolution, things in this Universe have gotten progressively more orderly. Evolution says that life started with a single-celled amoeba and "progressed" over millions of years into higher animals and eventually evolved into humans. But this idea cannot be made to fit the Second Law of Thermodynamics. Things are not getting progressively better, they are getting progressively worse.

||||||||||||||||||||||||||||||||||||||||||||||
The Second Law of Thermodynamics says that matter and energy are moving toward a less usable, more disorderly state called "entropy."
||||||||||||||||||||||||||||||||||||||||||||||

EVOLUTION'S COUNTER ATTACK

When faced with this problem, the evolutionist tries to wiggle away from the Second Law. For instance, he might say that the Second Law only applies to "closed systems" where no energy comes from an outside source. He would then say that our Earth is an "open system" since heat energy from the Sun hits our Earth all the time. But when he says this, he still has some serious

problems. First, no one has ever witnessed a real "closed system." Every system ever studied in nature has energy going out of it and into it, and yet the Second Law still works on every system we have ever seen. Second, is it true that simply by adding energy things **necessarily** get more complex and orderly? Absolutely not! Let's think about that.

Suppose we take all the parts needed to build a powerful laptop computer and put them in a shopping cart. If we leave them there for 5 years, will natural processes such as storms, wind, and rain assemble them into a working computer? No way! What if we left the pieces there for 50 years? Would more time help the pieces get any closer to a working computer? Absolutely not. In fact, the longer they stay there, the more worn out they will become. Well, maybe it is because we do not have enough energy. Now let's take that cart full of computer parts and put it in the middle of the desert where temperatures get well above the 100s. Will adding more sunlight (energy) help the parts assemble into a computer? No. In truth, the Sun will simply cause the parts to melt and get more disorderly. Adding more time or energy does not change the Second Law of Thermodynamics.

The Second Law of Thermodynamics is a natural law that disproves evolution. Not only that, it is exactly what the idea of creation predicts. In the beginning God saw everything that He had made and, indeed, it was very good. But since that beginning, things have been wearing out, exactly like the Bible writer stated: "You, Lord, in the beginning laid the foundation of the earth, and the heavens are the work of Your hands; they will perish, but You remain; and **they will all grow old like a garment**" (Hebrews 1:10-11).

Questions to Consider

✧ What are some other ways that you have seen the Second Law of Thermodynamics at work?

✧ Why does having more time not help the evolutionary scenario in light of the Second Law of Thermodynamics?

OUR WELL-DESIGNED PLANET

There is another problem with the Big Bang theory. When something explodes, it creates chaos and destruction, not order and design. For instance, if a person threw a stick of dynamite into a junkyard, would the explosion force lots of car parts together into a working car? No. In fact, an explosion in a junkyard would simply make those parts, which might have been usable, good for nothing. We know that explosions, unless engineered by an intelligent being, cannot produce order and design. When we look at the Universe, we find **design** that could not have come from a huge explosion like the Big Bang. When we examine the facts, it is obvious that God designed and built the Universe for us.

The Earth is 93 million miles from the Sun—a distance that happens to be just right for life to exist. The Sun is like a giant furnace, or nuclear engine. It gives off more energy in a single second than mankind has produced since the Creation. It converts 8 million tons of matter into energy **every single second**, and has an interior temperature of more than 20 million degrees Celsius. We should be glad we live so far from the Sun, because the 93 million miles of empty space between

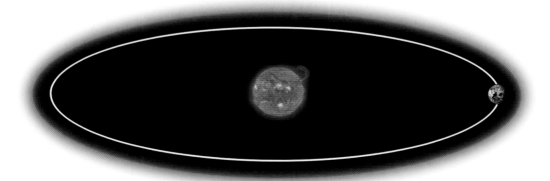

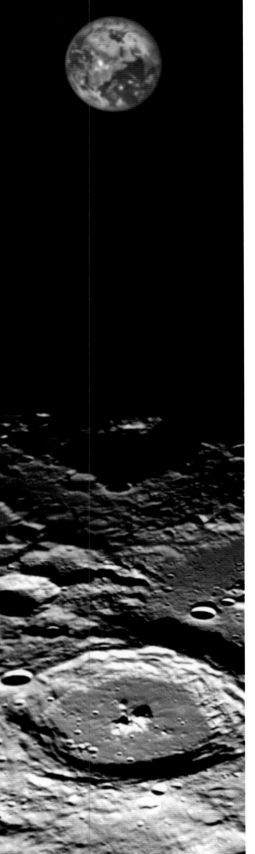

the Earth and the Sun help stop the destructive pressure waves given off by the Sun as it converts matter to energy. If the Earth were much closer to the Sun, people couldn't live because of the horrible heat and pressure.

The Sun also produces radiation, which is a form of light that can hurt our eyes, possibly give us cancer, and cause many other problems. Fortunately, humans receive some protection from this radiation because of a special gas known as "ozone." There is a layer of ozone in the Earth's stratosphere (about 12 to 18 miles up in the sky) that soaks up the radiation and keeps too much of it from hitting humans. In addition, the Sun constantly sends out an invisible wind that is composed of tiny particles called "protons" and "electrons." These particles approach the Earth from outer space at a very high speed, and could be very dangerous to humans. Instead, most of these protons and electrons are reflected back into space because God has made the Earth like a giant magnet that pushes away the solar wind and makes life on Earth possible.

The Earth is 240,000 miles from the Moon. This, too, is just right. The Moon helps control the movement of the oceans (tides). This movement is very beneficial to the Earth, because it provides a cleansing of shorelines, and helps ocean life to prosper. Tides are an important part of ocean currents. Without these currents, the oceans would stagnate, and the animals and plants living in the oceans and seas would soon perish. Our existence as humans depends upon the tides, which help to balance a delicate food chain in nature.

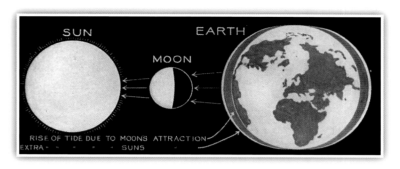

The Earth's oceans are another good example of perfect design. Water covers about 72% of the Earth's surface, which is good because the oceans provide a reservoir of moisture that constantly is evaporating and condensing. Eventually, this causes rain to fall on the Earth. It is a well-known fact that water heats and cools at a much slower rate than a solid land mass, which explains why deserts can be blistering hot in the daytime, and freezing cold at night. But water holds its temperature longer, and provides a sort of natural heating/air-conditioning system for land areas on the Earth. The Earth's annual average temperature (56°F; 13.3°C) is closely maintained by the great reservoir of heat found within the waters of the oceans.

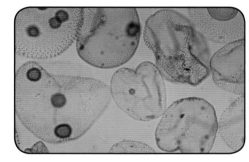

Tiny microscopic organisms like these produce 50% of the oxygen in our atmosphere.

Another well-known fact is that humans breathe in oxygen and breathe out carbon dioxide. Plants, on the other hand, take in carbon dioxide and give off oxygen. Humans depend on the plant world for a constant, fresh oxygen supply. But approximately 50% of that oxygen comes from tiny, microscopic plants within the Earth's oceans and seas.

The Earth's revolution around the Sun is exactly right, too. What would happen if the revolution rate of the Earth were halved, or doubled? If it were halved, the seasons would be doubled in their length, which would cause such harsh heat and cold over much of the Earth that it would be difficult, if not impossible, to grow enough food to feed the Earth's popu-

lation. If the revolution rate were doubled, the length of each season would be halved, and again it would be difficult or impossible to grow enough food to feed the people of the world.

The Earth is slanted on its axis exactly right. Its tilt is 23.5 degrees. If it were not tilted, but sat straight up in its orbit around the Sun, there would be no seasons. The tropics would be hotter, and the deserts would get bigger. If the tilt went all the way over to 90 degrees, much of the Earth would switch between very cold winters and very hot summers.

The Earth is balanced in a position, relative to the Sun, by gravity (which pulls the Earth toward the Sun) and centrifugal force (which pushes the Earth away from the Sun). As it travels in its orbit around the Sun (a distance of 600 million miles!), it moves at a speed of approximately 70,000 miles per hour, or 19 miles per second. But as it moves, it veers from a straight line only **one-ninth of an inch every eighteen miles**. If it veered by one-tenth of an inch, the orbit would become so large that life on the Earth would be impossible due to drastically reduced temperatures; if it veered by one-eighth of an inch, life on the Earth would be impossible due to drastically increased temperatures. Yet the Earth veers from a straight line only one-ninth of an inch, which is **just right**.

People who believe in evolution say that our Universe came into existence as the result of a "Big Bang" that accidentally caused the things we see around us. But the Earth is exactly the right distance from the Sun; it is exactly the right distance from the Moon; it has exactly the right tilt on its axis; it has exactly the right amount of water on its surface; it has exactly the

Extra Evidence

➤ The Earth's atmosphere is perfectly designed. If the atmosphere were much thinner, meteorites could strike our planet with greater force and frequency, causing worldwide devastation.

right amount of oxygen. And so on. Could all of these things be "just right"—**just by accident**?

Of course not! Instead, God is the One Who planned and designed the Universe. Moses said in Genesis 1:1, "In the beginning God created the heavens and the earth." The apostle Paul said it was God Who "made the world and everything in it" and Who "gives to all life, breath, and all things" (Acts 17:24-25). Moses and Paul both were correct. Our marvelous Universe can tell us a lot about our marvelous God—if only we will listen!

Freeman Dyson, a famous scientist (who does not believe in God) from Princeton University, once said that as he looked at the Universe and the Earth, he saw many things that he believed were the result of "accidents." But then he went on to say that when we see how these "accidents" have "worked together to our benefit, it almost seems as if the Universe must, in some sense, have known we were coming!" What?! Did the Universe (or the Earth) **know** that we were coming? Of course it did! The Bible tells us that God created this planet "to be inhabited" (Isaiah 45:18). In Acts 14:15, the apostle Paul told the people of his day that it was God "...who made the heaven, the earth, the sea, and all things that are in them." He also said that God "...did not leave Himself without witness, in that He did good, gave us rain from heaven and fruitful seasons, filling our hearts with food and gladness" (Acts 14:17). The Earth is our "just right" planet. Did it happen just by accident? No—it was designed by God. Let us give Him glory and honor for the wonderful place He has given us to live.

Freeman Dyson

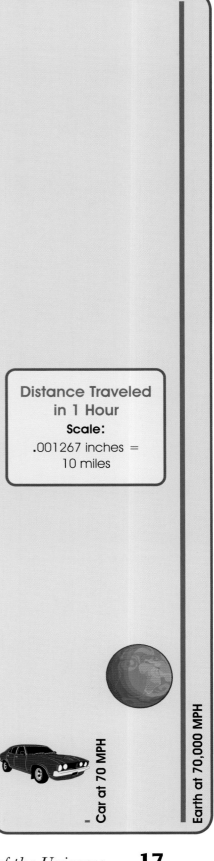

Distance Traveled in 1 Hour
Scale:
.001267 inches = 10 miles

Car at 70 MPH

Earth at 70,000 MPH

||||||||||||||||||||||||||||||||||||||||||||||||||||||||||||||||||||

"In the beginning God created the heavens and the earth."

Genesis 1:1

||||||||||||||||||||||||||||||||||||||||||||||||||||||||||||||||||||

CHAPTER REVIEW

FILL IN THE BLANKS

1. The Law of Cause and _____ states that every material effect must have an adequate antecedent cause.

2. _____ says that God "made the heaven, the earth, the sea, and all things that are in them."

3. Light travels _____ miles in one second.

4. Because everything in the Universe functions just right, we know that the Universe is a product of intelligent _____.

5. _____ says, "In the beginning God created the heavens and the earth."

6. The _____ _____ theory is used by some scientists to try to explain the origin of the Universe.

7. The _____ Law of Thermodynamics states that the Universe is constantly getting more disorderly.

8. The Earth is _____ miles from the Moon.

SHORT ANSWER

1. What is the Big Bang theory?

2. What does the Bible say about the origin of the Universe?

3. What is the First Law of Thermodynamics?

4. What is the Second Law of Thermodynamics?

5. If a scientific theory goes against a scientific law of nature, what should happen to the theory?

6. What is the Law of Cause and Effect?

7. About how many miles can light travel in a **year**?

8. Why does God not have a cause?

9. What is the difference between a scientific theory and a law?

10. What is entropy?

TRUE/FALSE

1. _____ Scientists make scientific laws.

2. _____ Every material effect must have an adequate cause that existed before it.

3. _____ When something explodes, it creates order and design.

4. _____ Our Universe is poorly designed.

5. _____ The Universe is gigantic.

6. _____ Our Earth is perfect for life.

7. _____ Our Earth is the result of an accident.

8. _____ The Big Bang is a proven scientific fact.

1. The Big Bang was said to have occurred how long ago?

   A. 100 years
   B. 140 years
   C. 14,000 years
   D. 14 billion years

2. What is entropy?

   A. A less usable, more disorderly state
   B. A more orderly state
   C. Heat
   D. An atmospheric gas

3. From nothing comes

   A. Nothing
   B. Something
   C. Everything
   D. Monkeys

4. What caused the Universe?

   A. God
   B. The Big Bang
   C. Nothing—we're just an accident
   D. The Universe does not exist

5. Things in the Universe are progressively getting

   A. Better
   B. Worse
   C. Neither A nor B
   D. Both A and B

6. Which law is BEST in explaining that nothing can exist forever in nature?

   A. Law of Conservation of Energy
   B. First Law of Thermodynamics
   C. Newton's First Law
   D. Second Law of Thermodynamics

7. How many miles away is the Earth from the Sun?

   A. 45 thousand
   B. 93 million
   C. 900
   D. 65 thousand

8. What causes ocean tides?

   A. Moon
   B. Mars
   C. Jupiter
   D. All of the above

9. Humans breathe

   A. In carbon dioxide, and out oxygen
   B. In carbon dioxide, and out nitrogen
   C. In oxygen, and out nitrogen
   D. In oxygen, and out carbon dioxide

10. The Earth is

    A. Exactly the right distance from the Sun
    B. Exactly the right distance from the Moon
    C. Exactly the right diameter
    D. All of the above

11. As the Earth orbits, it veers from a straight line

    A. 9 inches every 18 miles
    B. 9 feet every 4 miles
    C. 1 inch every 25 miles
    D. 1/9 of an inch every 18 miles

12. What does Exodus 20:11 teach?

    A. The Universe has always existed.
    B. The Earth was formed by a Big Bang.
    C. God created everything.
    D. The Universe created itself.

13. John 4:24 states that

    A. God was created
    B. God is Spirit
    C. God had a cause
    D. Energy can be created or destroyed

14. Our Universe displays _____ because everything works just right.

    A. Design
    B. Chaos
    C. Evolution
    D. The Big Bang Theory

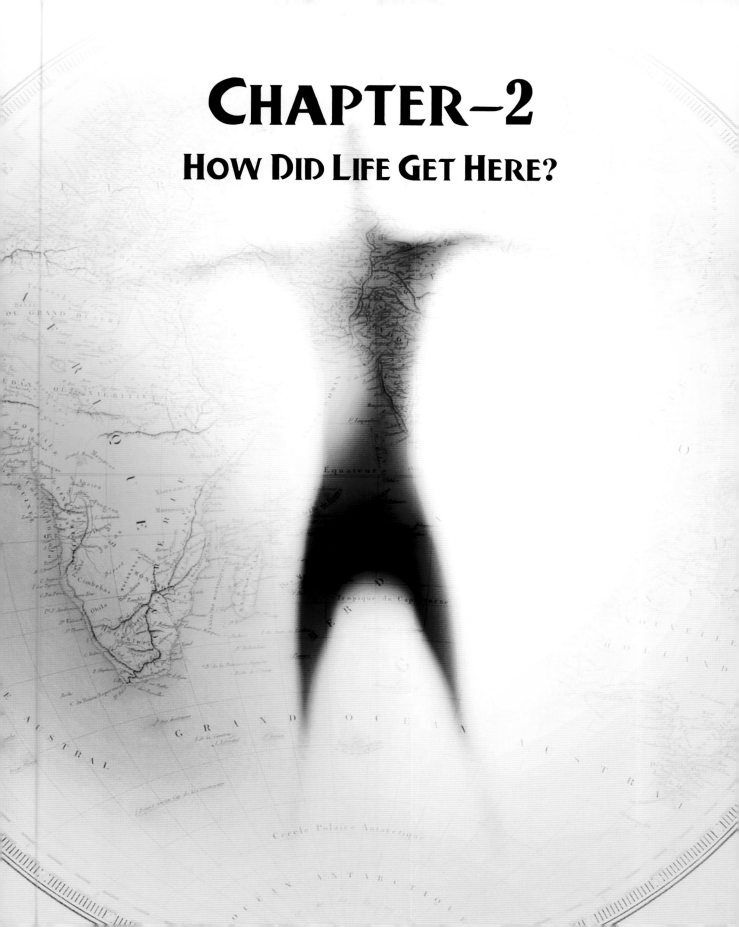

CHAPTER–2

HOW DID LIFE GET HERE?

When we look at the amazing world around us, we see many living things. There are cows, tulips, giraffes, lizards, canaries, polar bears, and humans—to mention just a few. Where did all of these things come from?

SPONTANEOUS GENERATION

Those who believe in the concept of evolution suggest that long, long ago on the Earth there was nothing living at all. But, eventually (so the story goes), something nonliving produced something living. Then, that first living thing changed into another living thing that was completely different. It, then, supposedly evolved into something else, which changed into something else, and so on. According to evolution, life originally came from nonlife (an idea known as spontaneous generation). And once life got started, one kind of plant gave rise to another kind of plant, one kind of animal gave rise to another kind of animal, and eventually, an animal gave rise to a human.

ORIGIN-OF-LIFE EXPERIMENTS

In order to "prove" that life can come from nonliving chemicals, scientists have tried to do experiments that produce life from nonlife. These experiments are often called "origin-of-life" experiments. One of the most famous origin-of-life experiments was performed by Stanley Miller and Harold Urey. Miller believed that lightning struck chemicals on the Earth millions of years ago. This electric charge supposedly was responsible for producing life out of the chemicals. So, Miller and Urey built a miniature "world" with certain chemicals in it, but nothing that was living. They also made a place in the experiment where a spark would strike the chemicals. After the spark struck the chemicals, they made a place to catch whatever formed. After sending water and chemicals through the apparatus, they "caught" several interesting things. Mostly, they caught a sticky dark tar. But they also found that certain amino acids had formed. Amino acids form proteins, and proteins can form life. After repeating the experiment, they found that some of the amino acids needed for life could form. Certain people who believed in evolution said that Miller and Urey had "proved" that life could have come from nonliving chemicals.

But there were several problems with the experiment. First, it did not form life. It produced only tiny building blocks that, under the right conditions, can form life. That would be like trying to build a new building out of a bunch of chemicals. After shocking those chemicals, you produce clay that sometimes can be formed into bricks—and bricks can be used to construct a building. Have you proved that you can erect a building from a bunch of chemicals? No. All you have proved is that those chemicals can form clay. It takes a very intelligent person to form clay into bricks, and it takes

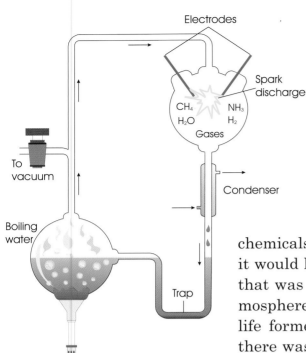

Electrodes

Spark discharge

CH₄ NH₃
H₂O H₂

Gases

To vacuum

Condenser

Boiling water

Trap

an even more intelligent person to form bricks into a building.

Miller and Urey also had another problem. Oxygen is a chemical that makes up about 21% of our atmosphere. We need oxygen to live. Animals and humans must breathe oxygen to survive. But Miller and Urey did not put any oxygen in the experiment. Why not? Because oxygen is a chemical that breaks down other chemicals. If they had put oxygen in the experiment, it would have immediately destroyed every amino acid that was formed. Today, we know that the Earth's atmosphere contained oxygen when evolutionists think life formed (supposedly billions of years ago). Yet, if there was oxygen in the atmosphere, all the amino acids needed for life would have been destroyed. Miller and Urey knew that oxygen would ruin the experiment, so they did not use it. Their experiment did not prove that life comes from nonliving chemicals. In fact, it proved just the opposite. Life could **not** have evolved in an environment that contained oxygen (like that on the early Earth).

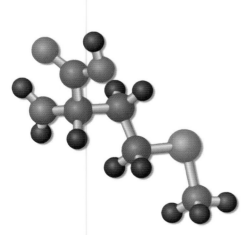

Here is something else to think about. Stanley Miller, Harold Urey, and other scientists doing similar experiments are very intelligent people. They have spent thousands of hours trying to form life from nonliving chemicals. They have not even come close to accomplishing their goal. Yet, they believe that in nature, life came from nonliving chemicals by accident. It has taken them thousands of hours to try to produce life, and they have failed. Does it make sense to believe that it happened **by accident** in nature? If these intelligent people who are trying to pro-

duce life cannot do it, why should we believe that "nature" somehow accidentally produced life? The truth is, God created living things during the six days of Creation. Life did not form slowly over millions of years. And life did not accidentally pop up out of non-living chemicals.

THE LAW OF BIOGENESIS

As scientists study nature, they observe that certain things happen with astounding regularity. One of the things that happens regularly is that living things always come from other living things. Scientists have known this for many years. In 1858, a German scientist by the name of Rudolph Virchow stated it like this: "Every cell arises from a preexisting cell." In 1860, Louis Pasteur, a famous French scientist, said: "Every [biological] living thing arises from a preexisting living thing."

Two very famous experiments were done in the past that helped to disprove the false idea of spontaneous generation. These experiments also helped scientists to identify the Law of Biogenesis (by-oh-GEN-uh-sis). The first experiment was done by an Italian scientist named Francisco Redi, who lived from 1626-1698. In his day, many people believed that life spontaneously generated from nonliving things. One of the most common ideas was that maggots spontaneously generated from meat. The proof offered for this was that if meat was left sitting out for a time, maggots would form. Redi did not believe that maggots spontaneously generated. He believed that flies landing on the meat caused the maggots. In order to test his idea, he did a series of experiments, which took place in 1668. He put meat in several jars. Some of the jars

he left open so that flies could land on the meat. Some of the jars he completely sealed so that no air or flies could get to the meat. Other jars he covered with a netted fabric like our medical gauze. As he expected, maggots formed only on the meat that the flies could contact. No maggots formed in the sealed or covered jars. His experiments proved that maggots did not spontaneously generate.

Although Redi's experiments were helpful with the idea of maggots, many people continued to believe that tiny, microscopic germs could form from nonlife. Around the year 1860, a brilliant scientist named Louis Pasteur dealt the deathblow to the theory of spontaneous generation. He did a series of experiments in which a liquid was boiled in a special flask. The flask had a long S-shaped curve designed to let air in, but to trap any organisms in the bottom of the curve. After boiling the liquid, no organism grew because of the specially designed flasks. Pasteur proved once and for all that germs and bacteria are carried through air, and do not spontaneously generate. Today, liquids like milk are "pasteurized" (heated to kill microorganisms) using the same idea that Pasteur used to disprove spontaneous

Louis Pasteur

Before Pasteur's groundbreaking experiments, tiny microscopic organisms were believed to have spontaneously generated.

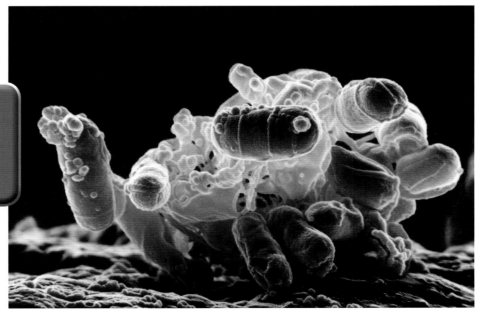

generation. The next time you see a carton of milk, look on the side to see if it is pasteurized. (It is!)

These scientists of the past were proving what scientists of today call the Law of Biogenesis. This law says two things: (1) living things always come from living things; and (2) living things produce only more living things like themselves. In nature, we never have seen a single exception to this basic law of science. For example, to get a cow, you must first have a living thing. But, that living thing cannot be a horse, a donkey, or a whale. It must be a cow. To get a rose, you must have a living rose. To get a lion, you must have a living lion. That is what the Law of Biogenesis says. And remember—there are **no exceptions** to this scientific law.

Evolution is in disagreement with this law. Evolutionists tell us that living things in nature came from nonliving matter. They also tell us that one kind of animal gave rise to a different kind of animal. But that would violate a known law of science!

The Bible makes it clear that life did not originate in this fashion. Rather, living things on the Earth were created by a living God Who is supernatural, which means that He is outside of nature. Genesis 1:20-25 states:

In nature we have never seen a single exception to the Law of Biogenesis.

One reason that evolution cannot be true is because it goes against the Law of Biogenesis.

Then God said, "Let the waters abound with an abundance of living creatures, and let birds fly above the earth across the face of the firmament of the heavens." So God created great sea creatures and every living thing that moves, with which the waters abounded, according to their kind, and every winged bird according to its kind.... Then God said, "Let the earth bring forth the living creature according to its kind: cattle and creeping thing and beast of the earth, each according to its kind"; and it was so. And God made the beast of the earth according to its kind, cattle according to its kind, and everything that creeps on the earth according to its kind.

The Law of Biogenesis is not make-believe; it is real. It is a law observed everyday in nature. One reason that evolution cannot be true is because it goes against this law.

CHAPTER REVIEW

FILL IN THE BLANKS

1. _____ is a chemical that makes up about 21% of our atmosphere.
2. Francisco _____ was an Italian scientist who lived from 1626-1698.

SHORT ANSWER

1. What are "origin-of-life" experiments?
2. What two things are stated in the Law of Biogenesis?
3. What term is defined as life coming from nonlife?

TRUE/FALSE

1. ____ Evolutionists believe in the idea of spontaneous generation.
2. ____ Miller and Urey proved that something can come from nothing.
3. ____ Amino acids are the building blocks of proteins.
4. ____ Creation agrees with the Law of Biogenesis.
5. ____ A cow can evolve into a horse.
6. ____ Evolutionists can prove there are exceptions to a scientific law.
7. ____ The Law of Biogenesis is the opposite of spontaneous generation.
8. ____ Creationists believe that humans were formed by a chemical explosion.
9. ____ Scientists have been trying to create life from nonlife for years.
10. ____ God created living things during the six days of Creation.

MULTIPLE CHOICE

1. Stanley Miller and Harold Urey
   A. Attempted to create life from non-living chemicals
   B. Invented the atomic bomb
   C. Were the 39th President and Vice President of the United States
   D. Were great Gospel preachers

2. Stanley Miller and Harold Urey believed that chemicals came to life many years ago as a result of
   A. A meteor crash
   B. A tornado
   C. A lightning strike
   D. An earthquake

3. What did Miller and Urey not include in their experiment?
   A. Carbon
   B. Nitrogen
   C. Selenium
   D. Oxygen

4. A fact in science that is true and has been proven
   A. Law
   B. Theory
   C. Hypothesis
   D. Experiment

5. What would have happened if oxygen had been put into the Miller and Urey experiments?

    A. Life would have formed.

    B. The amino acids would have formed proteins.

    C. They would have created a human.

    D. All the amino acids would have been destroyed.

6. What were the results of the Miller and Urey experiments?

    A. They proved that living organisms could be created from nonliving material.

    B. They did form amino acids, but did not prove that organisms could be created by nonliving material.

    C. They could not even form the building blocks of life from the nonliving chemicals.

    D. The results did not convince evolutionists that life could have come from nonliving chemicals.

7. Which two scientists claimed that living things come only from living things?

    A. Stanley Miller and Isaac Newton

    B. Stanley Miller and Rudolph Virchow

    C. Louis Pasteur and Rudolph Virchow

    D. Louis Pasteur and Stanley Miller

8. The law which states that every biological living thing arises from a pre-existing living thing is called the

    A. Law of Gravity

    B. Law of Biogenesis

    C. Second Law of Thermodynamics

    D. Napoleonic Code

9. What is the relationship between evolution and the Law of Biogenesis?

    A. Evolution is in harmony with this law.

    B. Evolutionists teach this law.

    C. Evolutionists invented this law.

    D. Evolution is in disagreement with this law.

10. Genesis 1:20-25 states that God made

    A. Birds

    B. Sea Creatures

    C. Every living thing that moved

    D. All of the above

11. This makes up about 21% of the Earth's atmosphere

    A. Carbon

    B. Oxygen

    C. Nitrogen

    D. Ammonia

12. This scientist disproved that maggots spontaneously generate from meat

    A. Louis Pasteur

    B. Stanley Miller

    C. Albert Einstein

    D. Francisco Redi

CHAPTER–3

WHAT IS EVOLUTION?

Charles Darwin, 1809-1882

CHANGES: BIG AND SMALL

The word "evolution" can have many different meanings. Basically, the word means "to unroll, unfold, or change." Anything can "evolve" or change over a period of time. For instance, the body style of the Corvette® certainly has "evolved" since the 1960s. Young children "evolve" into adults. A bud can "evolve" into a flower. However, when most people think of evolution, they do not think about small changes, such as in the design of a car, the growth of children into adults, or the development of a bud into a flower. In the present day, the word evolution brings to mind thoughts of an amoeba gradually changing over millions of years into a human.

So, in order to determine whether or not evolution is true, we must clarify what kind of "change" we are discussing.

amoeba

Small changes in living things are recognized and accepted by both creationists and evolutionists. Such changes have been given the name "microevolution," meaning "small change." Microevolution is responsible for much of the diversity that we see in dogs, cats, and other animals. However, even though through the years people figured out how to breed different dogs to create the particular variety of dog they want, no one has ever figured out how to breed two dogs together and get a cat. Small changes do occur within limits, but eventually those changes come to a genetic barrier that is impossible to cross.

Both evolutionists and creationists recognize the fact that small changes do take place in plants and animals. However, some

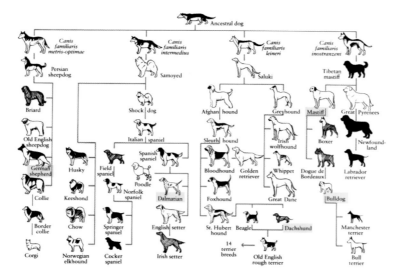

Small changes do occur, but eventually those changes come to a genetic barrier that is impossible to cross.

people refuse to recognize that these changes have certain limits. They believe that if nature is given enough time, then it will eventually turn a dog into something other than a dog. This idea of "big change" is often called "macroevolution" (also known as the "General Theory of Evolution"). This idea basically states that all living things originated from a single life form billions of years ago. Then, by a series of changes over billions of years, this life form "evolved" into different creatures such as fish, lizards, monkeys, and man.

The problem with "macroevolution" is that it goes against what we have observed in nature, in that it does not recognize the **limits** of change. No one has ever seen a dog produce anything other than a dog. Sure, a long-eared dog with a long tail and long legs can have a puppy with short ears, a short tail, and stubby legs. But the puppy will always be a dog.

CHARLES DARWIN'S THEORY

Charles Darwin

Charles Darwin, often referred to as "the father of evolutionary theory," did not always believe in evolution. In fact, at one point in his life he believed in God as Creator. But as he grew older, he changed his view and began to think that natural forces, not God, created this world. One of the reasons for his change in thinking came from a misunderstanding of the Bible. In Darwin's day, the Church of England misunderstood the biblical account of Creation. The book of Genesis says that animals reproduce "according to their kind" (Genesis 1:21). That means that an elephant will always give birth to a baby elephant, and a finch will always give birth to a baby finch. However, the Church of England confused the biblical word "kind" with the biologists' word "species." The Church of England taught that God had created every different species in the world—an idea that came to be known as "fixity of species." The problem with this view was that it simply was not true; people had misunderstood what the Bible said. When Darwin went on a trip around the world to study nature, he discovered that animals within a species are not fixed, but can (and do) change. He looked closely at nature, and rejected the incorrect idea of "fixity of spe-

cies" based on the factual evidence that he found. Darwin was wrong, however, to go beyond the facts and refuse to recognize that change has built-in limits. If the Church of England had not misunderstood the Bible, then things might be different today. Let this be a lesson to all of us. We all must study the Bible so we can properly understand it and teach it, and we must be honest with the facts of nature. When both are correctly understood, they will not disagree.

FINCHES OF THE GALÁPAGOS ISLANDS

Charles Darwin loved to look at nature. In fact, he was invited on a trip aboard a ship called the H.M.S. Beagle that traveled around the world. His job was to be a naturalist—a person who looks at different kinds of animals and plants. In 1835, Charles Darwin and his shipmates traveled to the Galápagos Islands. All sorts of strange, exotic creatures lived on these islands. Huge tortoises and swimming iguanas were just a few of them. Also on these islands there lived several different kinds of finches. The different finches looked very similar to each other, except for the fact that they had different-sized bodies, and their beaks were different sizes and different shapes. Today, there are said to be about thirteen different species of finches on the Galápagos Islands, but Darwin had found only nine species of the finches, and he thought that only six of them were really finches.

The H.M.S. Beagle in the Straits of Magellan, 1832. Darwin had the job of naturalist on this ship. His 5-year voyage of exploration would take him around the world, including the Galápagos Islands.

The story that you will read in many science books goes something like this. Darwin supposedly looked at the different species of finches, and noticed how similar they were. He thought that all of the finches must have originally come from one kind of finch. A long time before he came to the island, so the story goes, a storm blew a flock of finches away from the

mainland and onto the islands. Some of the finches in the flock had beaks better suited to eating large seeds. Other finches had beaks better suited for eating small seeds. Finches with similar beaks stayed together, because they ate the same kind of food. Eventually, the one flock became about thirteen different kinds of finches. According to most science books that tell this story, these finches influenced Darwin to believe in evolution.

The true story, however, is much different from that. Darwin collected only nine species of finches, and he thought only six of them were finches. In fact, in Darwin's famous book, *The Origin of Species*, he did not even mention the finches. When he first saw the finches, it seems that Darwin did not think they provided evidence for evolution.

Many years after his trip to the Galápagos Islands, and after writing his book, Darwin began to think about the finches again. If nature could change the size and shape of a finch's beak in a few years, what could nature change in a few **million** years? Could nature turn the finch into a different animal? He began to think that the finches might be good evidence of evolution. In

Questions to Consider

◇ Does the fact that finches can have changes in their beak or body size prove that they could evolve into animals other than a finch?

◇ How are these small changes in the animal kingdom accounted for in the Creation model? [Hint: Consider God's ability to foresee His creatures' needs.]

Large ground-finch (left) and warbler finch (right)

The only thing that "Darwin's finches" prove is that a finch always stays a finch!

fact, many school textbooks today teach that "Darwin's finches" are a good example of evolution. But it turns out that "Darwin's finches" are not good evidence for evolution at all!

First, no one can prove that the finches came from the same flock. Even though the finches look very similar, they might have all been different in the first place. No one knows if a flock of finches ever really was blown by a storm to the Galápagos Islands.

Second, every kind of creature in the world has built-in limits in its genetics. The finches might have larger beaks, and the finches might have smaller beaks, but the finches always had beaks. The finches' beaks did not change into a muzzle with teeth. Their beaks did not change into a scaly, lizard-mouth. For the past 160 years, people have been studying the finches on the Galápagos Islands, and those finches have always had beaks.

Third, the finches never changed into anything other than finches. Even if all the species did come from one flock, they are still finches. None of them has changed into a crow, a snake, a dolphin, or a dog. For over 160 years, the finches have changed into...more finches! The only thing that "Darwin's finches" prove is that a finch always stays a finch!

Darwin collected pigeons like kids collect baseball cards. He was fascinated by the varieties or "sports" that man had bred. If man could do so much in a short time, he thought, then there were no limits to what nature could do over a long time. This idea has not been proven by science.

NATURAL SELECTION

The Origin of Species by Means of Natural Selection was the main title of Charles Darwin's book, first published in 1859. Those last two words, "natural selection," have been discussed often in the halls of science. And it is no secret that Darwin's concept of natural selection (or "survival of the fittest," as it has come to be known) has been at the center of evolutionary thought.

According to Darwin, a creature with a particular advantage—the "fittest of its kind"—would be "naturally selected" to pass on the advantage to its offspring. A horse with long legs, for example, would be able to gallop faster than the rest, thus escaping from wolves or other predators in order to produce other baby horses with long legs. A "fit" creature, therefore, was one that could best carry out the functions that kept it alive, and made it best adapted to its environment. This is what Darwin meant by "survival of the fittest."

But problems with the theory of natural selection soon developed. Somehow, natural selection was supposed to ensure the "survival of the fittest," but the only realistic way to define the "fittest" was "those that survive." Basically, then, natural selection simply says that all the winners win, and those who win are the winners. Natural selection does not explain **how** those creatures came to be the most "fit."

Creationists have never objected to the idea of natural selection as a way that gets rid of unfit, poorly adapted organisms. As a matter of fact, creationists long before Darwin said that natural selection was a good conservation principle (think of it as a screening device for getting rid of the unfit). If a harmful mutation causes a grasshopper to have only one leg, then that grasshopper will be an easier meal for a bird. Natural selection is the Creator's plan for preventing harmful mutations from destroying an entire species. But natural selection cannot cause one kind of animal or plant to "evolve" into another kind of animal or plant. In reality, it is nothing more than an argument that reasons in a circle. As one scientist said, "[N]atural selection can account for the **survival** of the fittest, but it cannot account for the **arrival** of the fittest."

GENETIC MUTATIONS

If you have ever seen a one-eyed cat, a two-headed calf, or a five-legged frog, you have witnessed a mutated animal. A mutation is a permanent change in the genetic material of an organism. Whereas most cats, calves, and frogs have one head, two eyes, and four legs, altered DNA (deoxyribonucleic acid) within the nuclei of cells can cause living organisms to look very different from other animals of the same kind, including their parents. Although a child's parents may have brown skin, if the child's gene for skin color is mutated, he may be born without color in his skin, eyes, and hair. This mutation is known as albinism (which comes from a Latin word meaning white).

Suppose that a certain gene's DNA sequence is represented by the following sentence made up of three-letter words:

The big cat ate the owl and the dog ate the pie.

This sentence (representing a gene) is clearly understandable. Every letter functions perfectly for its intended purpose. However, if the sentence mutated so that the first letter attached itself to the end of the sentence (or gene) rather than the beginning, you would

> ||||||||||||||||||||||||||||||||||||||||||||
> **Natural selection is the Creator's plan for preventing harmful mutations from destroying an entire species.**
> ||||||||||||||||||||||||||||||||||||||||||||

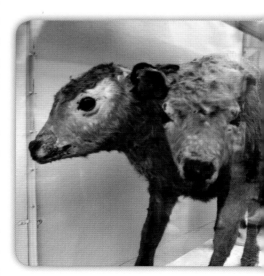

Normal Vision

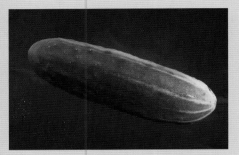

Protanope (1 in 100 males)

Deuteranope (5 in 100 males)

Color blindness is a common genetic mutation in males. Six percent of males, but only ½ a percent of females, are born with some form of it. These images simulate what a color blind person may see when looking at an everyday item.

simply have a line of jumbled letters (representing a mutated gene).

Heb igc ata tet heo wla ndt hed oga tet hep iet.

These groups of letters no longer communicate a clear thought. One letter changed position, and the entire sentence was altered. Similarly, if the genetic information in a living organism is changed ever so slightly, mutations can form. Color blindness, albinism, and sickle cell anemia are all examples of mutations.

So what do mutations have to do with creation and evolution? At the turn of the century, just as Darwin's idea of natural selection was beginning to fall on hard times, the science of genetics was born. Some who began to study genetics felt that they had found the actual mechanism of evolution—genetic mutations. The new idea then became that species arose by mutations that (somehow) were plugged into the system by natural selection. Today, the supposed mechanism of evolution is natural selection **plus** genetic mutations (since natural selection by itself has no power to create anything).

Evolution without a mechanism is like a car with no engine—it is not going anywhere. Evolutionists soon realized that natural selection **alone** was not a good enough mechanism. Organisms would not (and could not!) change from one species to another unless the genetic material—the DNA—was changed. Mutations are genetic changes passed from parent to offspring.

The only possible mechanism of evolution is natural selection plus genetic mutations. We are told that "nature" has "selected" certain beneficial mutations and plugged them into various organisms, eventually causing those plants or animals to change from one kind to another. But there are some very serious problems with this idea. Consider, for example, the following.

1. **Mutations are random.** There is no way to control mutations or to predict with accuracy when they will occur. In other words, nature is not "selecting" at all. Rather, "nature" is forced to accept whatever appears. The obvious question, then, is: What appears?

2. **Mutations are very rare.** How often do random mutations occur? One scientist said: "It is probably fair to estimate the frequency of a majority of mutations in higher organisms between **one in ten thousand and one in a million** per gene per generation." Evolutionists themselves admit what every research biologist knows: mutations occur rarely, and when they do, they are entirely random.

3. **Good mutations are very, very rare.** In theory, there are at least three kinds of mutations: good, bad, and neutral. Obviously, the bad mutations (causing various diseases and death) are not what the evolutionist needs. Neutral mutations are of little use as well, since they are neither harmful nor helpful. So the question really is: How often do **good** mutations occur? Hermann J. Muller, an award-winning scientist in the field of genetics, said: "Accordingly, the great majority of mutations, certainly well over 99%, are harmful in some way, as is to be expected of the effects of accidental occurrences."

Even many evolutionists admit that mutations are mostly destructive and cannot provide a reasonable mechanism for evolution. Furthermore, mutations simply change something that already exists. Mutations do not create anything new, but only alter what is already there. Mutations can cause a fly to have six wings, a fish to have three eyes, or a person to have an abnormal face, but they cannot create a fly or fish or person—no matter how much time is available. Natural selection plus mutations still does not answer the question of life's origin and development.

Color blindness, like most mutations, is not beneficial. Looking at the two traffic lights above, it is easy to see how it could be difficult for a person to drive on city streets with the most common form of color blindness.

Powerful Point

☑ Remember, mutations do not create genetic information, they only alter existing information. Mutations cannot account for the origin of living things.

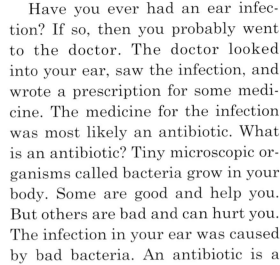

Have you ever had an ear infection? If so, then you probably went to the doctor. The doctor looked into your ear, saw the infection, and wrote a prescription for some medicine. The medicine for the infection was most likely an antibiotic. What is an antibiotic? Tiny microscopic organisms called bacteria grow in your body. Some are good and help you. But others are bad and can hurt you. The infection in your ear was caused by bad bacteria. An antibiotic is a substance that kills bacteria. That is why it helped get rid of your infection.

But some bacteria build up a resistance to antibiotics. Genetic mutations can cause the bacteria to change slightly so that antibiotics no longer work on them. People who believe in evolution claim that bacteria that build up resistance to antibiotics prove that evolution is true. They believe these small changes in bacteria prove that bacteria could evolve over billions of years into a human.

People who use small changes in bacteria to "prove" evolution have several problems. First, the bacteria change a little, but they always stay the same type of bacteria. For instance, a bacterium called *E. coli* has changed in many small ways, but it has always been *E. coli* and has never changed into another kind of organism. It has never evolved into part-bacterium and part-fish or part-lizard. The fact that bacteria stay the same kind of bacteria is exactly what you would expect if God created them and commanded them to multiply after their own kind.

Second, most of the mutations that change bacteria are not helpful. The mutations might help the bacteria live when attacked by an antibiotic, but in the long run, they hurt the bacteria. For example, suppose that a certain kind of bacteria has something like a right hand and a left hand. And suppose that an antibiotic kills the bacteria by attaching itself to the left hand of the bacteria. Then imagine that the bacteria mutates so that it loses its left hand. The antibiotic cannot kill the bacteria any longer, but the bacteria now has only one hand. "One-handed" bacteria might be resistant to antibiotics, but they are "crippled" and do not survive long. The fact that some bacteria become resistant to antibiotics certainly does not prove the bacteria could evolve into humans.

Even though bacteria can change in small ways, these changes do not prove evolution. In fact, they do just the opposite. They prove that bacteria remain bacteria, exactly as God instructed them to do during the Creation week.

> **Bacteria remain bacteria, exactly as God instructed them to do during the Creation week.**

THE FLY THAT STAYS A FLY

Imagine looking at a table covered with jars. Each jar contains several fruit flies. Some of the flies have no wings, some have tiny, useless wings, and others have several pairs of wings. Other jars have flies with legs growing out of their heads where antennas should be. Some of the flies are yellow, others are black. Some of the flies have 25 bristles, others have 50 bristles. Some of the flies have red eyes, others have orange eyes, and others have no eyes at all. What is going on?

The common fruit fly, called *Drosophilia melanogaster*, is often used by scientists to study mutations. Since the flies can breed new flies every

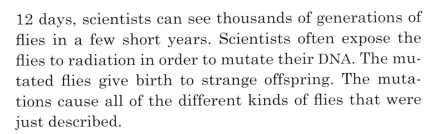

The fruit fly has proven that evolution is false.

12 days, scientists can see thousands of generations of flies in a few short years. Scientists often expose the flies to radiation in order to mutate their DNA. The mutated flies give birth to strange offspring. The mutations cause all of the different kinds of flies that were just described.

Some scientists hoped that speeding up the mutation rate of the fruit fly would help them learn how evolution works. In fact, scientists have studied fruit flies for almost 100 years and have seen millions of generations. But the fruit flies have not shown scientists how evolution works—because evolution does not work.

The fruit fly has proven that evolution is false. Even after millions of mutated generations, the fruit fly has not evolved into anything else. There are no half-fly/half-birds. There are no flies that have mutated into lizards or half-mice. In fact, the fruit fly shows that mutations cannot combine to form a kind of animal different from the original animal.

The result of the research on fruit flies is exactly what you would expect if the fly was created by God. In the first chapter of Genesis, God told the animals and plants to be fruitful and multiply **after their own kind**. The fruit fly has been multiplying after its own kind in science labs all over the world for many years. It has never changed into another kind of creature, even though scientists have caused it to mutate every way they possibly can. It is amazing how such a small creature can provide so much important evidence for creation!

CHAPTER REVIEW

FILL IN THE BLANKS

1. _____ is a type of evolution that refers to small changes.

2. _____ _____ is referred to as the "father of evolutionary theory."

3. Natural selection plus _____ _____ is the supposed formula for macroevolution.

4. _____ _____ spent time studying as a naturalist on the H.M.S. Beagle.

5. _____ _____ was supposed to ensure the "survival of the fittest."

6. _____ is a type of evolution that deals with large changes.

7. The Church of England taught that God had created every different species in the world—an idea that came to be known as the _____ __ _____.

8. Many science textbooks say that _____ _____ are a good example of evolution.

9. Darwin's book that explained his views on macroevolution was titled _____ _____ _____ _____.

10. A _____ is someone who looks at different kinds of animals and plants.

TRUE/FALSE

1. ____ Microevolution means "large change."

2. ____ Creationists recognize the fact that small changes do take place in plants and animals.

3. ____ Genetic change has limits.

4. ____ Good genetic mutations are common.

5. ____ An elephant will always give birth to an elephant.

6. ____ Darwin does not mention finches in *The Origin of Species*.

7. ____ The supposed mechanism of evolution is natural selection plus genetic mutations.

8. ____ Mutations are rare.

9. ____ Mutations merely change something that already exists.

10. ____ Natural selection plus mutations answers the question of life's origin and development.

SHORT ANSWER

1. Briefly describe the differences between macroevolution and microevolution.

2. Why are genetic mutations not able to cause the origin of species?

3. According to most science books, what influenced Darwin to believe in evolution?

4. Explain how research on fruit flies has proven evolution to be false.

1. What is another term for the "General Theory of Evolution"?
   A. Microevolution
   B. Macroevolution
   C. Spontaneous generation
   D. Genetic mutations

2. Who is often referred to as the "father of evolutionary theory?"
   A. Charles Darwin
   B. Martin Luther
   C. Louis Pasteur
   D. Thomas Edison

3. The Church of England in Darwin's day misunderstood the biblical word "kind" in Genesis 1:21 as meaning _____.
   A. Gracious
   B. Loving
   C. Species
   D. Compassion

4. Which incorrect idea of the Church of England did Charles Darwin reject?
   A. General Theory of Evolution
   B. Original Sin
   C. Baptism
   D. Fixity of species

5. On what islands did Darwin observe nature?
   A. Galápagos Islands
   B. Hawaii
   C. Madagascar
   D. Japan

6. What bird was Darwin famous for observing?
   A. Eagle
   B. Finch
   C. Mockingbird
   D. Woodpecker

7. What book did Darwin write that outlined his theories on the evolution of life?
   A. *Alice in Wonderland*
   B. *Evolution Revolution*
   C. *The Origin of Species*
   D. *The Last of the Mohicans*

8. The mechanism for evolution is supposed to be natural selection plus _____.
   A. Creation
   B. Biblical science
   C. Genetic mutations
   D. Natural disasters

9. The result of the research on fruit flies is exactly what you would expect if
   A. Flies evolved from lower life forms
   B. Flies evolved from non-life
   C. Mutations can cause evolution
   D. God created flies after their own kind

10. Goats on a farm having less hair than wild goats is an example of
    A. Microevolution
    B. Macroevolution
    C. Both of the above
    D. None of the above

11. Mutations are
    A. Random
    B. Rare
    C. Rarely beneficial
    D. All of the above

CHAPTER–4
DESIGN DEMANDS A DESIGNER

HELLO CLASS

Suppose you were sitting at your desk in school, and your teacher stood before the class and announced that she had a very special guest to introduce to the class. You were expecting to see a new student, but when the door opened, it was not a new student. It was a robot. The robot was the size of a normal fifth-grade boy. It had arms and legs, and walked with a jerky motion. It walked to the front of the class and said, "Hello, class."

Your teacher said that this was the latest robot designed by a panel of brilliant scientists. The robot, named Chip (for the amazing microchip in its head), had the ability to be programmed with over 40 different languages. It could answer questions and store lots of information. Your teacher urged you to ask Chip some questions. Lucy, the girl sitting in front of you, asked, "What is the speed of light?" Chip answered: "Approximately 186,317.2 miles per second." The class was amazed. Billy raised his hand and asked, "Why did the chicken cross the road?" Billy was the class clown. Chip did not understand the question. Your teacher explained that robots cannot really understand humor or jokes. At the end of class, your teacher said that Chip cost 18 million dollars to make, and "he" took several brilliant scientists nearly 10 years to complete.

Now suppose that on another occasion you were sitting at your desk in school, and your teacher stood before the class and once more announced that she had a very special guest to introduce to the class. This time it was a new student. The student's name was Cindy. She was from California. She said hello to the class and even understood Billy's joke. She did not walk with a jerky motion, and

Questions to Consider

◇ What other things can the human body and mind do that robots and computers cannot do?

◇ What are some characteristics which prove that design exists in the Universe? [Hint: You may want to refer back to chapter 1.]

she was not "manufactured" by scientists. She was an "ordinary" fifth grader.

Let's think about that for a moment. The robot was designed by brilliant scientists over several years, but he could not even understand a joke. Cindy was a normal fifth grader who could do many more things than Chip. Yet, those who believe in evolution want you to believe that your body was not designed. They want you to think that it accidentally evolved over millions of years by chance. That does not make sense. If the robot was designed by brilliant scientists, then the human body, which can do much more than any robot, had to be designed. In this chapter, you will learn all about the amazing design of the body, and you will learn about God, the amazing Designer.

The human body is much better than any machine that has ever been designed. First, the body is made up of cells, which are the smallest unit of life. Second, the body contains tissues (like muscle and nerve tissue), which are groups of the same kind of cells that perform the same kind of activity. Third, groups of tissues working together make up organs like the heart, liver, and lungs. Fourth, there are systems (such as the reproductive system and the circulatory system), which are made up of groups of organs carrying out specific bodily functions. In the following pages, you will learn how these cells, tissues, organs, and systems show God's design.

Cells

Tissues

Organs

Systems

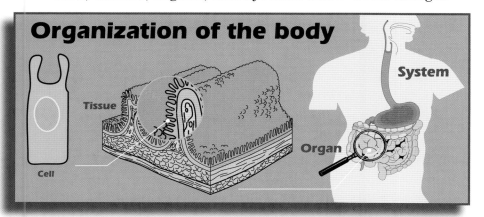

Organization of the body

Tissue

System

Organ

Cell

THE CELL

There are many amazing things in this Universe. But surely one of the most amazing is the cell. Just think about it. Cells come in a variety of different shapes and sizes. Cells may be shaped like rods, spirals, daisies on their stalks, string beans, shoeboxes, or snowflakes. Some cells can be quite large, like the yolk of an ostrich egg. Others can be quite small. For example, 20,000 human body cells could fit inside a capital "O" from a typewriter. Some cells live very long lives. Nerve cells in a human can live over 100 years! Some cells have very short lives. Platelets (which help blood to clot) live less than 4 days.

Cells are beautifully organized and extremely complex. Each human cell is able to communicate with other cells, dispose of waste, reproduce, feed, and repair itself. Some areas of the cell produce proteins, which are carried to other parts of the body. Some areas of the cell produce the energy that your body needs to work, think, or play. Still other areas of the cell are responsible for what we call reproduction—the process by which cells make more cells.

Each cell has a cell membrane that surrounds it. Inside the cell there is cytoplasm—a watery substance containing specialized organelles. Organelles are like tiny machines in the cell that do different jobs. Inside the cytoplasm is the nucleus, which serves as the control center of the cell.

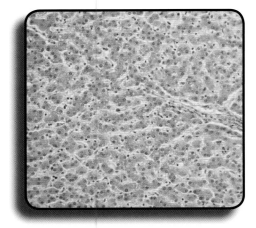

Inside the cytoplasm, there are over 20 different chemical reactions occurring at any one time, with each cell containing components for five major functions: (1) communication; (2) waste disposal; (3) nutrition; (4) repair; and (5) reproduction. Within this watery substance, there are organelles such as the mitochondria (over 1,000 per cell in many instances) that provide the cell with its energy. Other organelles called ribosomes are miniature protein-producing factories. Golgi bodies store the proteins manufactured by the ribosomes, while lysosomes function as waste-disposal units. You could picture the lysosomes like garbage men on a big trash truck, making sure the trash can at your house gets emptied.

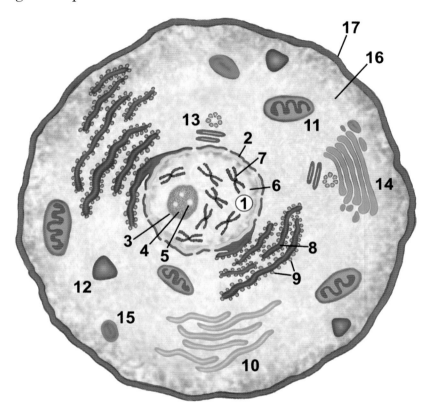

1. Nucleus
2. Nuclear envelope
3. Nucleolus
4. RNA and proteins
5. Nucleoli
6. Chromatin
7. DNA packaged in chromosomes
8. Rough endoplasmic reticulum
9. Ribosomes
10. Smooth endoplasmic reticulum
11. Mitochondria
12. Peroxisome
13. Centrioles
14. Golgi
15. Lysosomes
16. Cytoplasm
17. Cell membrane

Deep inside the cell is the nucleus, which contains the "genetic code." This code is a set of instructions inside each cell that tells the cell to become a fingernail, a hair, an eye, a bone, or some other part of the body. These instructions are very complicated, and are placed in the cell in a chemical that scientists call DNA (a short way of saying deoxyribonucleic acid). The DNA in a single human cell is about 3 feet long and contains over 6 billion "steps." If all the DNA in a single human body were stretched out end-to-end, there would be over a billion miles' worth.

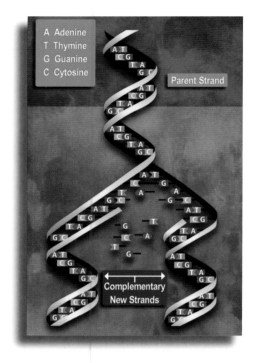

A Adenine
T Thymine
G Guanine
C Cytosine

Parent Strand

Complementary
New Strands

Also, the DNA molecule does something amazing: it stores coded information. Then it uses RNA (ribonucleic acid) to decode the information. If the information in the DNA were written in English, the DNA in a single human cell would fill a 300-volume set of encyclopedias of approximately 2,000 pages each. We all recognize that not a single book in a library "just happened." Each and every book is the result of intelligence and design. If each book had an intelligent designer, then we know that DNA must have been designed. What is more, all the genetic information needed to reproduce the entire human population (about six billion people) could be placed into a space of about one-eighth of a cubic inch.

The writer of the book of Psalms said to God, "I will praise You for I am fearfully and wonderfully made" (139:14). Our bodies—composed of 60-100 trillion cells—are wonderful! Could evolution have produced cells, or bodies composed of cells, by accident? No! The Bible says, "For every house is built by someone; but He Who built all things is God" (Hebrews 3:4). Cells speak loudly to us about how great and powerful our God is.

The genetic code of DNA in a single human cell would fill a 300-volume set of encyclopedias if written out.

THE BRAIN

You see a leaf—and you think of a tree. You hear "meow"—and you think of a cat. You smell chocolate—and you think of a candy bar. You touch an ice cube—and you think of a freezer. You taste cinnamon—and you think of homemade cinnamon rolls.

Where do all these thoughts of trees, cats, candy bars, and cinnamon rolls come from? They are memories that are stored in your brain. There is plenty of room in there for lots more memories. Scientists tell us that the brain can hold as much information as 500 sets of encyclopedias!

How big is your brain? When you were a baby, your brain weighed less than a pound. By the time you were 6 years old, your brain reached its full weight—almost 3 pounds. The brain may be small, but it is very important. It is so important that it is protected in three ways. First, there is the skull, or cranium, which is composed of 2 layers of hard bone. Second, there is fluid all around the brain. The brain floats in this fluid, which helps absorb shocks if the head gets hit. Third, on the outside of the brain there is a covering called the dura mater. Those are the Latin words for "hard mother." It is called the dura mater because, like a mother, it is very protective.

Thoughts and memories travel through your brain's cells as slow as 3 miles an hour and as fast as 300 miles an hour. Yet, for all its amazing work, the brain produces only about 20 watts of electricity—not even enough to power an average light bulb!

Brains are divided into two halves (called hemispheres). As strange as it may sound, the right side of your brain normally controls the left side of your body; the left side normally controls your right side. Scientists think that the hemispheres also perform different

"I will praise You for I am fearfully and wonderfully made" (Psalm 139:14).

tasks. Things like the ability to recognize words and remember names are controlled by the left hemisphere. Emotions, the ability to sing, and the ability to judge distance are the kinds of things controlled by the right hemisphere.

The brain is connected to the spinal cord, which runs down our back. Together, the brain and spinal cord are called the "central nervous system." It is in charge of all our movements, controls such things as breathing and heartbeat, and is responsible for incoming and outgoing messages to and from our eyes, ears, nose, and other organs.

The brain also produces more than 50 chemicals, and dispenses them as they are needed. In a sense, your brain contains its own doctor and pharmacist. When needed, "Dr. Brain" prescribes the right medicine and dispenses it. Here are a few examples: endorphins (en-DORF-ins) are powerful painkillers; serotonin (sare-uh-TOE-nin) affects our moods (like depression); dopamine (DOPE-a-mean) can make us excited and talkative.

Extra Evidence

➤ Though the brain makes up only 2 percent of the average person's body weight, it consumes 25 percent of the body's oxygen, and receives 20 percent of all the blood that is pumped from the heart.

Some scientists who do not believe in God, but who believe in evolution instead, say that the brain "just happened." The brain is too well designed and too complicated to have "just happened." The brain is one of the most orderly and complex arrangements of matter in the entire Universe. Could this order and complexity have evolved by accident? No! When we—with our brains—think about the brain, we see more and more of God's great wisdom and power.

THE EAR

Rain falling on the roof. The bark of a dog. The singing of "America, the Beautiful." The voice of your mother as she tells you she loves you. Laughter. What do all these things have in common? They are all things you hear. But how do you hear?

Sounds cause "wave patterns" that travel through the air. Different sounds cause different wave patterns. A cat's meow is not the same as a guitar string being plucked. As sound waves enter our ears, they bounce off what we commonly call "eardrums." These eardrums inside the hearing canal vibrate (move)—sometimes fast, sometimes slow—depending on how loud the sound is.

Farther inside the ear, in what is called the "middle ear," are three tiny bones: the hammer, the anvil, and the stirrup (funny names for bones inside an ear, wouldn't you say?).

These bones receive vibrations from the eardrum, and amplify (increase) them so they then can be sent to the snail-shaped cochlea (COCK-lee-uh), which has 25,000 tiny hair cells. In the cochlea, the vibrations are changed into electrical signals, which go to the brain through the auditory nerve. When the brain receives the signals, it sifts through its filing cabinet of memories and matches the incoming sound with one already recorded.

All of this takes place in a fraction of a second! Pretty amazing, isn't it? In order to hear, a long chain of events has to occur, and yet it has to be "compacted" into a fraction of a second so our body can respond almost instantly to a train whistle, or a friend's cry for help, or a mother's "Don't do that!" The ear certainly shows a lot of beautiful design. But some scientists insist that it

Hammer Anvil Auditory Nerves

Hearing Canal Eardrum Stirrup Cochlea

Chapter—4 *Design Demands a Designer* **55**

"evolved." When we see a telephone, we know it had a designer. If the ear is more complicated than the telephone (and it is!), could it have "just happened" by evolution? No! If it has design, it must have had a designer. That Designer is God.

THE EYE

The human eye is one of the most complicated mechanisms in the world. Even Charles Darwin admitted that it is hard to believe that this magnificent device could arise accidentally. The eye gathers over 80% of the information that is transmitted to the brain. Each eye is connected to the brain by over 600,000 nerves that send messages to the brain at 300 miles an hour! Scientists tell us that the eye receives 1.5 million messages at the same time, sorts through them, and sends them to the brain. The retina covers less than a square inch and contains about 137 million light-sensitive receptor cells, 130 million rods (allowing the eye to see in black and white), and 7 million cones (allowing the eye to see in full color).

In an average day, the eye moves about 100,000 times, using muscles that, milligram for milligram, are among the body's strongest. The body would have to walk 50 miles to exercise the leg muscles an equal amount.

The eye is self-cleaning. Lacrimal glands produce tears to flush away dust and other foreign materials. Eyelids act as windshield washers. The blinking process (3-6 times a minute) keeps the sensitive cornea moist and clean. And, tears contain a potent microbe killer (lysozyme) that guards the eyes against bacterial infection. During times of stress,

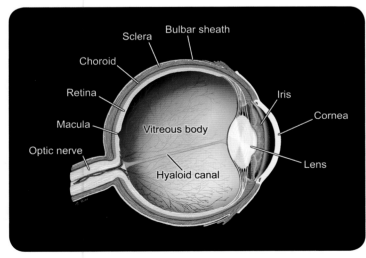

Sclera
Bulbar sheath
Choroid
Retina
Iris
Macula
Cornea
Vitreous body
Optic nerve
Lens
Hyaloid canal

one eye will rest while the other does 90% of the work; then the process is reversed, allowing both eyes equal amounts of rest. In fact, the eye works so well that technological companies model cameras after it. Today, we have tiny camcorders that can be held in one hand and be used in both bright and dim light. They have lenses, an automatic focus, color monitors, and a host of other well-engineered features that allow them to record images. Yet, even with all the time, effort, and money that went into designing these technological jewels, they are but clumsy copies of the human eye. If we found a camcorder lying on the ground, who would say that it "just happened" by chance? And yet the average human being has two eyes that make the camcorder look like a kindergartner's toy. If we are looking for design, truly the eyes have it.

THE HEART

Inside your body there are about 80,000 miles of blood vessels, which make up a network that is longer than any single railroad system in the United States. Your heart (an organ about the size of a man's clenched fist) works hard every day to make sure that the proper amount of blood is sent throughout the body. About 5 quarts of blood are pumped through the heart every minute (around 7,200 quarts every day). Yet, for all the pumping that your heart does, it rests about 6 hours each day. If you live to be 60, your heart will have rested almost twenty years. And it needs that rest, because it does enough work every minute to lift a 70-pound weight one foot off the ground. By the end of the day, your heart has done enough work to lift your body one mile straight into the air.

This mega-muscle beats about 75 times per minute in the average human. In a hundred-year period, it will have faithfully beaten 4 billion times and sent 600,000 tons of blood through the body. That blood makes a complete cycle from heart to the lungs, back to the heart, through the body, and then back to the heart in about one minute. And yet, some people expect us to believe that this efficient machine came about through random processes and blind chance.

If you compare an artificial heart (which took thousands of hours to design, millions of dollars to build, and hundreds of experiments to test) with a human heart, which is more efficient? Which would you rather have beating in your chest? Absolutely no question about it—humans have the heart of design!

BIOMIMICRY

In the world of technology and science, a new field of study has become quite popular. It is called "biomimicry." The word biomimicry comes from two Greek words: *bios*—meaning "life," and *mimesis*—meaning "to imitate." Therefore, biomimicry means the imitation of life. This field of study looks at certain things in nature, and attempts to use the designs and structures found there to create technology that is helpful to humans.

THE FLY: THE FIGHTER JET OF THE ANIMAL KINGDOM

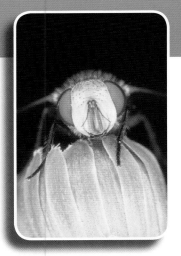

The list of things included under the term biomimicry is very long. Scientists have begun to develop a tiny flying robot that mimics a fly. Interestingly, it is about the same size and weight of a fat housefly. Many uses have been proposed for this "robofly," including helping firefighters locate people during fires or spying on potential terrorists. Why would anyone want to copy a fly? The reason is very simple; flies are some of the most well-designed flyers in the world. Ron Fearing, the scientist behind much of the research on the robofly, said that flies are "the fighter jets of the animal world." They can change speed and direction in a fraction of a second, and they can even land upside down. Just try catching one with your hand to see how great they are at flying. Dr. Fearing went on to say, "There are all kinds of things nature can do that we don't know how to do yet."

VERSATILE VELCRO®

Have you ever been outside when it was really cold—and your tennis shoes came untied? Remember how hard it was to re-tie them with frozen fingers? Or, have you ever tried, with just one hand, to button a shirt sleeve on your opposite arm? Wouldn't it be neat if someone invented an easier way to make things "stay put"?

Well, someone has! God provided the idea in nature in what we know as a cocklebur, which is a plant seed that has tiny hooks. When these hooks touch a piece of your clothing, they stick to it very tightly! In 1948, a man from Switzerland named George de Mestral was walking his dog. When they returned to the house, both were covered with cockleburs. Mr. de Mestral wanted to know why the cockleburs stuck like they did. When he put one under the microscope, he saw the tiny hooks—which gave him an idea.

He decided to try to copy the tiny hooks, and then make something to which they could stick—just like they did to his clothes (and his dog!). Eventually, he invented what we know today as Velcro®. [He came up with the name Velcro® by combining the two French words for "velvet" (*velour*) and "hook" (*crochet*).] Where did George de Mestral get his idea for this amazing "hook and loop" combination? From a cocklebur! And who created the cocklebur? Nature's Great Designer—God—Who also created you!

THE SILK "STEEL" OF A SPIDER

Pound for pound, the silk from certain kinds of spiders is five times stronger than steel, and is twice as strong as the material that currently makes up SWAT teams' bulletproof vests. It can stretch 30 percent farther than the stretchiest known nylon, and is twice as flexible. Scientists have even discovered that spider silk can stretch 40 percent beyond its original length without breaking. In fact, due to its amazing strength and stretchiness, it has been said that you could trap a jumbo jet with spider silk that is the thickness of a pencil. To top it all off, the silk from spiders is waterproof.

Although spiders give most of us the creeps, these little creatures are on the cutting edge of technology. Their silk is made up of chains of amino acids (protein)—an arrangement that is responsible for the silk's amazing strength. Since scientists have found it too difficult to "outdo" what God created in the beginning, they have decided instead to try and use God's special critters and the silk "steel" they produce.

Can you imagine how useful it would be if we could produce our own spider silk? We could make soft, lightweight, bulletproof vests for policemen—vests that would absorb five times the impact of current ones. Scientists believe spider silk will one day be found in everything from non-tear sports jerseys, air bags, and fishing line to artificial tendons used by doctors to repair an athlete's torn ligament.

COLD LIGHT

Have you ever tried to unscrew a light bulb from a lamp that has been on for 10 or 15 minutes? We don't recommend that you attempt this, but if you have, you know that your standard light bulb gets very hot very quickly—and remains hot the whole time it is on. The average bulb lights up when the tiny filament inside is heated by the electricity that passes through it. Unfortunately, heat and light bulbs go hand in hand. About 95% of the energy produced by a light bulb is lost in the form of heat. For this reason, scientists have sought new ways to produce cheaper and safer forms of light.

One "new" form of light involves chemical reactions (without the addition of heat). You probably have seen this kind of light in the form of glow sticks (or light sticks). People like them so much because they produce light without heat (and they look pretty cool, too!). What people seem to overlook is that this technology really isn't new. Man did not invent this kind of light. It actually has been here since the Creation when God made lightning bugs. Lightning bugs (also called fireflies) are little beetles that carry their own "flashlights." These insects have special chemicals called luciferin (lew-SI-fer-in) and luciferase (lew-SI-fer-ace), which they combine with oxygen to form a bright, heatless light. This process is called bioluminescence (by-oh-LOO-meh-NESS-sense)—the emission of light from living organisms.

For years scientists have studied fireflies in hopes of learning how they produce "cold light," and they have been somewhat successful. But scientists confess that light from fireflies (and certain other bioluminescent creatures) still is many times more efficient than what they can produce in laboratories.

The more scientists learn about the little beetle we call a firefly, the more amazed they are at its complexity. Sadly, many of these same scientists believe that the firefly simply evolved over millions of years—from who knows what. They dismiss both its obvious design and the Great Designer Who created it.

Many of the people who study biomimicry say that all these wonderful designs and structures are the result of evolution, but that does not make any sense. If humans, who are very intelligent, have not been able to create designs and structures as efficient as those in nature, then how could evolution have done it by blind chance and accident? Doesn't it make much better sense to think that God, the great Designer of the Universe, created these amazing designs? Isn't it amazing how God's design—found in a common housefly, cocklebur, spider, or firefly—is better than some of the technology found in our most advanced jet planes? The apostle Paul had it right when he said that "the foolishness of God is wiser than men, and the weakness of God is stronger than men" (1 Corinthians 1:25).

CHAPTER REVIEW

FILL IN THE BLANKS

1. _____ _____ produce tears to flush away dust and other foreign materials.

2. _____ means the imitation of life.

3. _____ stores coded information using chemicals.

4. The part of the cell that contains the genetic code is the _____.

5. _____ are like tiny machines in the cell that do different jobs.

6. The DNA molecule uses _____ to decode its information.

7. The hammer, anvil, and stirrup are the bones found in the _____.

8. The brain and spinal cord make up the _____ _____ _____.

9. The _____ is a watery substance inside the cell that contains specialized organelles.

10. The snail-shaped organ of the ear in which vibrations are changed into electrical signals is called the _____.

11. George de Mestral created Velcro® after examining the _____.

12. Goose bumps help to prevent _____ _____.

13. "The foolishness of God is _____ than men, and the weakness of God is _____ than men" (1 Corinthians 1:25).

14. The name _____ comes from two French words for "velvet" (*velour*) and "hook" (*crochet*).

TRUE/FALSE

1. ____ There are 75,000 cones in the ear.

2. ____ The eyes produce several different kinds of drugs for the body to use.

3. ____ On the outside of the brain there is a covering called the *alma matrix*.

4. ____ The brain produces enough energy to power an average light bulb.

5. ____ The ability to sing is controlled by the right hemisphere of the brain.

6. ____ The heart rests about 6 hours each day.

7. ____ Charles Darwin believed that God designed the eye.

8. ____ The heart pumps 5 quarts of blood per minute.

9. ____ There are 80,000 miles of blood vessels in your body.

10. ____ Spider silk has some amazing qualities.

11. ____ In nature we cannot see any design.

12. ____ Design in the Universe demands some type of designer.

13. ____ Ribosomes are part of the cell.

14. ____ The word "biomimicry" means to copy man-made structures.

1. What are the protein producers of the cell?

   A. Ribosomes

   B. Lysosomes

   C. Nucleus

   D. DNA

2. Which one of these is not a part of the cell?

   A. Golgi bodies

   B. Lysosomes

   C. Sebaceous gland

   D. RNA

3. The brain is protected by which of the following

   A. Skull

   B. Fluid

   C. *Dura mater*

   D. All of the above

4. The brain is able to prescribe all of the following drugs except

   A. Ibuprofen

   B. Endorphins

   C. Dopamine

   D. Serotonin

5. Where are the hammer, anvil, and stirrup bones located?

   A. Eye

   B. Knee

   C. Middle ear

   D. Arm

6. What is the name of the snail-shaped organ in the ear containing 25,000 tiny hair cells?

   A. Eardrum

   B. Cochlea

   C. Stirrup

   D. Auditory nerve

7. Each eye is connected to the brain by over 600,000 nerves that send messages to the brain at _____ miles per hour.

   A. 80

   B. 120

   C. 300

   D. 560

8. What part of the eye contains 137 million light-sensitive receptor cells, 130 million rods and 7 million cones?

   A. Pupil

   B. Iris

   C. Lens

   D. Retina

9. Inside your body there are about _____ miles of arteries, veins, and capillaries.

   A. 80,000

   B. 2

   C. 10

   D. 1000

10. What skin muscles cause hairs to stand on end?

    A. Biceps

    B. Arrector pili

    C. Gastrocnemius

    D. Hair follicle

11. What field of study looks at certain things in nature, and attempts to use the designs and structures found there to create technology?

    A. Hydrology

    B. Archaeology

    C. Astronomy

    D. Biomimicry

CHAPTER–5
GEOLOGY AND THE FOSSIL RECORD

THE GEOLOGIC COLUMN

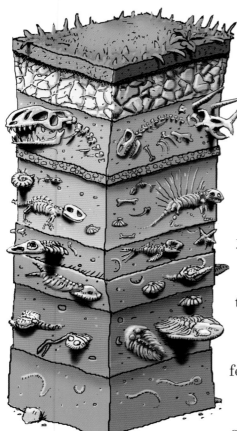

In art class or during craft time, maybe you have done sand art. Using a glass jar and several different colors of sand, you begin to pour the sand into the jar one color at a time. Then you might take a long, sharp utensil like a pencil and run it down the side of the jar to make the colors zig-zag into pretty shapes. Naturally, the first color of sand you pour into the jar is on the bottom; the second is next to it; the third is on top of that, and so on.

Did you know that if you could look at the Earth in a jar, you would see layers similar to the ones in your sand art? You can see some of these layers when you look at the Grand Canyon. Scientists call these layers the geologic column. Geology is the study of the Earth, which is why these layers are called the geologic column.

In these layers of the Earth we find millions of different fossils. Evolutionists teach that the "simplest" organisms are found in the "oldest" layers at the bottom of the geologic column, while more "complex" organisms are found in "younger" layers at the top. They

call this idea the "law of superposition," which basically says that the layers on the bottom are the "oldest" layers while the layers on the top are the "youngest" layers. Evolutionists also teach that the layers were laid down over millions of years, and that the fossils found in the layers represent plants and animals that evolved during that time in Earth history.

But neither of these teachings is true. In fact, the idea that these layers were laid down over long periods of time, that they contain organisms in a "simple-to-complex" order, and that they somehow "prove" evolution, has some serious problems. This chapter will show you some of those problems. For instance, some plant and animal fossils cut through several layers. Does that mean that these plants or animals were being fossilized over millions of years? Also, those animals that look "simple" aren't as simple as some people once thought. Trilobites (sea-living animals with a shell that can be found in the lower layers of the column) had more complex eyes than most of the "complex" animals found above them. How could the plants and animals be progressing from "simple to complex" if the ones on the bottom were already complex?

Another problem with this idea of long ages of time has to do with the Flood of Noah. Think back to your sand art. Imagine dumping water into the jar very quickly and shaking it up really hard. When it settled out, would the bottom still be the sand that you poured in first? Probably not. Those who look at the geo-

How could the plants and animals be progressing from "simple to complex" if the ones on the bottom were already complex?

logic column and say it took millions of years to form do not even consider the great Flood of Noah.

When we examine the geologic column more closely, we find that it gives some good evidence for Creation. For example, if evolution were true, then we would expect to see many half-and-half, or transition fossils (such as a half-reptile/half-mammal) gradually changing from one kind of animal into another. But what we really find are millions of plants and animals that are fully formed and that appear in the column with no gradual line of fossils before them—which is exactly what you would expect to find in a world that was created!

Transitional creatures showing a clear progression from one kind of animal to another have never been found in the fossil record, neither have they been discovered living in nature. The links that are supposed to show how one kind of animal evolved into another are still missing. Animals like the one in this picture have never existed.

POLYSTRATE FOSSILS

Embedded in rocks all over the globe are "polystrate" fossils. Polystrate means "many layers," and refers to fossils that cut through at least two layers of the geologic column. For example, geologists have discovered tree trunks buried vertically in two, three, four or more sections of rock—rock that evolutionists suggest was deposited over millions of years. In Nova Scotia, there are many erect fossil trees scattered throughout layers extending upward more than 2,500 feet. However, organic material (like wood) that is exposed to the elements will rot, not fossilize. Scientists have had to admit that the trees must have been preserved quickly, which suggests that the layers surrounding them must have been deposited rapidly. The rock layers did not build up slowly over millions or billions of years.

Geologists also have discovered polystrate animal fossils. Probably the most famous is the fossilized skeleton of a whale discovered in 1976 near Lompoc, California.

The whale is covered in "diatomaceous [die-uh-toe-MA-shus] Earth." Diatoms are microscopic algae. As diatoms die, their skeletons form deposits—a process that evolutionists say is extremely slow. But the whale (with a skull more than seven feet thick) is completely covered by the diatomaceous earth. There simply is no way the whale could have remained on its back for hundreds of years while diatoms covered it, because it would have decayed or been eaten by scavengers. It is clear

Most animals or plants that are not buried quickly are eaten by scavengers, or decay without being fossilized.

from this extraordinary evidence that the long ages attached to the geologic column simply are not correct.

Trees, whales, fish, and the other organisms with which the fossil record abounds did not die and lie around for hundreds, thousands, or millions of years while slowly being turned into polystrate fossils. Truth be told, polystrate fossils testify loudly to a young Earth whose layers formed rapidly—and not very long ago.

TRILOBITES

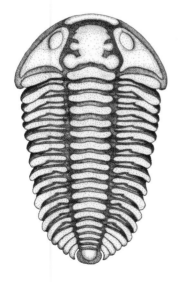

Many years ago, scientists discovered fossils of animals resembling small horseshoe crabs that once lived in the ocean (supposedly over 250 million years ago). They named these creatures trilobites (TRY-la-bites), meaning "three-lobed," because their bodies were divided lengthwise into three sections. There were several thousand different kinds of trilobites. While some grew to be as much as a foot long, most were only a few inches in length.

While these creatures possessed many fascinating characteristics, none was more fascinating than their compound eyes, which some scientists have called "the greatest living lenses." The trilobites' eyes were different than most creatures' eyes because they were composed of materials that could be studied even after being fossilized. Most creatures' eyes dissolve after death; trilobites' eyes did not. When scientists began studying these eyes, they were amazed at what they found.

Humans have only one lens in each eye. But trilobites had two lenses in each of their many eyes. In order to see clearly under water, it was necessary for them to have this "double lens" in each eye. If their eyes did not have two lenses, things probably would have appeared very distorted. The scientists discovered that the lenses were so perfect that there would have been no distortion at all. Their eyes were so "perfect" they looked as if they had been—designed!

Since trilobites are considered to have been one of the first creatures to evolve, it would make sense (from an evolutionary point of view) to suggest that they possessed fairly primitive features. Yet the eye of the trilobite is anything but primitive! How could this "perfect eye" be found in an "early" animal like the trilobite? And how could it have been so well designed? People who believe in God know the answer: evolution is wrong. The trilobite's eye did not evolve. It was designed by God. Only He could make "the greatest living lens."

||||||||||||||||||||||||||||||||||||||||||||||

The trilobite's eye did not evolve. It was designed by God. Only He could make "the greatest living lens."

||||||||||||||||||||||||||||||||||||||||||||||

EVIDENCE THAT TRILOBITES AND HUMANS ONCE LIVED AT THE SAME TIME

Evolutionists teach that trilobites became extinct more than 250 million years before man appeared on Earth. They are so certain that these creatures lived nearly one-quarter-of-a-billion years ago that they even consider trilobites to be "index fossils." This means that if evolutionists find a fossil (from an unknown time) near a trilobite, then the unknown fossil automatically is assumed to be at least 250 million years old.

In 1968, however, a man in Utah named William Meister discovered a footprint of a human wearing a

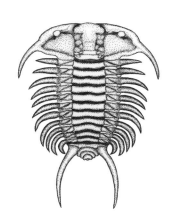

shoe. Although he was somewhat surprised to find the shoe print, he was much more surprised at what he found inside the print. Mr. Meister found fossilized trilobites in the toe and heel of the shoe print. This extraordinary evidence from the geologic column shows us that evolutionists are wrong. Trilobites are not separated from humans by 250 million years. Both the Bible and true science agree that humans and trilobites once lived upon the Earth at the same time (Exodus 20:11).

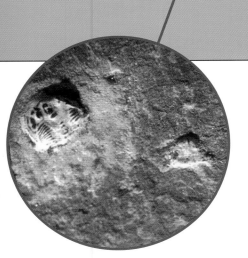

WHERE ARE THE "MISSING LINKS"?

According to Charles Darwin, evolution took place over many millions of years. He thought that living things slowly and gradually changed little by little. He also thought that half-way animals (like a half-lizard/half-bird) should be found in the fossil record. These "half-way" animals that he thought should be in the fossil record are called transitional forms. They are called transitional forms because Darwin thought certain kinds of animals were making a transition (changing) into other kinds of animals. Mr. Darwin believed that millions of these transitional forms should be found in the fossil record. What if they were not there? He said that if these transitional fossils were not in the fossil record, then it would be a serious problem for his theory.

Were there transitional fossils during Darwin's day? No. He and the other scientists who were studying his theory did not find the transitional fossils that they thought should be in the fossil record. When Darwin tried to give an answer for this, he said that they were missing because of the incompleteness of the fossil record. He hoped that in time, after scientists dug up more fossils, they would find many of these transitional fossils.

Charles Darwin

That was in 1859. Today, we have been digging up fossils for more than 145 years. In fact, we have discovered so many fossils, we do not even have room to display them in museums. If evolution is true, we should have an enormous number of fossils that show one type of animal changing into another type of animal. The truth is, however, we do not have fossils that show a clear transition from one kind of animal into another. Fossils that are put forth as transitional fossils eventually are proven not to be transitional at all. Consider the coelacanth and *Archaeopteryx*.

THE COELACANTH

For decades, evolutionists taught that coelacanths (SEE-la-kanths) became extinct about the same time dinosaurs did (supposedly 65 million years ago). In the past, it was said that these fish gradually developed legs and began to live on land, and then sometime later became extinct. Evolutionists thought that these fish were the "missing link" between certain water and land animals. Similar to the ape-like creatures that allegedly evolved into humans, these fish were said to have evolved into land animals millions of years ago. In fact, evolutionary scientists used the coelacanth as a part of their "index fossil" system, meaning that any rocks that contained coelacanth fossils were considered to be at least 65 million years old (with other fossils in those rocks assumed to be at least that old as well).

Until 1938, evolutionists believed that men and coelacanths could not possibly have lived at the same time. These creatures were known only from the fossils that evolutionists claimed were millions of years old. But then, on December 24, 1938, the scientific world was "rocked" when an unidentified fish, 5 feet long and weighing over 100 pounds, was brought to shore in South Africa. It was caught in the Indian Ocean near Madagascar. The fisherman who netted the fish (having no idea what the creature's proper name was) called it "the great sea lizard" because its pectoral fins looked more like little fringed legs. Once scientists examined this strange creature, however, they confirmed what formerly was thought impossible—a coelacanth had been caught in modern times! One evolutionist said that he could not have been more surprised if he had come across a living dinosaur. After all, according to their theory, coelacanths evolved before dinosaurs and became extinct about the same time dinosaurs did.

Since 1938, over 100 coelacanths have been caught. In 1952, they were seen swimming near the Comoro Islands in the Indian Ocean. Another population was found in 1998 off the coast of Indonesia. Surprisingly, local Indonesian fishermen were quite familiar with this fish, having been catching them for years, though scientists were totally unaware they lived in that region.

Modern-day coelacanths look like their fossil counterparts (which are mistakenly dated as being millions of years old). The fact that these modern-day creatures have stayed the same as their fossilized ancestors is no surprise to Christians. The Bible teaches that animals produce "after their kind" (Genesis 1:21,24), and the fossil record proves that this is exactly what has happened. Fish never gradually devel-

oped over millions of years into land animals, any more than ape-like creatures developed into humans.

What makes the evolutionary idea about coelacanths being a missing link even more outrageous is that these fish live near the ocean floor. Scientists now know that the coelacanth is a deep-water fish that rarely comes within less than 500 feet of the surface. So, even if there was a missing link between fish and land animals (and you can be sure that there was not), since these fish hardly ever swim near the water surface (and close to land), they could not have been the missing link.

In reality, coelacanths have always been coelacanths—nothing more and nothing less. Their discovery in modern times makes a mockery of evolutionary dating methods, and takes us back to the time of the dinosaur, which was not all that long ago.

In 1939, Professor J.L.B. Smith of Rhodes University in England offered a reward to those who could catch a coelacanth.

ARCHAEOPTERYX

Among the many thousands of birds of the world, there is amazing variation. Some birds are very small (like tree sparrows); others are very large (like buzzards). While some birds fly many thousands of miles every year (like Arctic terns), others cannot fly at all (like New Zealand kiwi birds).

Some birds that God created no longer live (they are extinct). One of the most unusual birds that is now extinct is called *Archaeopteryx*. Even though *Archaeopteryx* had feathers and was about the size of a crow, controversy has surrounded this creature for a long time because it also had some features that are similar to a small dinosaur. *Archaeopteryx* had teeth in its beak and claws on its wings. Because of such characteristics, some evolutionists believe that this animal was a link between reptiles and birds, and supposedly is proof that birds evolved from dinosaurs. Evolutionists tell us that the claws and teeth of *Archaeopteryx* suggest that it had been a reptile in the past.

Actually, however, such characteristics of *Archaeopteryx* do not prove that it was the missing link between reptiles and birds. Consider the following evidence:

- Some modern birds have claws on their wings, but no one thinks of them as being missing links. The hoatzin of South America has claws when it is young, which it uses to climb trees. (The stamp on the next page highlights these claws.) The touraco of Africa also has claws. And if you have ever seen an ostrich close up, you might have noticed that it has three claws on each wing that it can use if attacked. The presence of "claws" says nothing about its ancestry.

- Fossil studies have shown that other true birds, which are now extinct, also had teeth. And so, the presence of teeth does not mean that *Archaeopteryx* was a dinosaur-bird link.

- This strange bird also had feathers, just like birds today, and the feathers were fully formed. *Archaeopteryx* did not have half scales/half feathers, but fully formed feathers. It was not in some kind of in-between stage.

> **Animals did not slowly evolve from one kind into another.**

- It also is known that there were other true birds living at the same time as *Archaeopteryx*. In fact, scientists have even found fossilized birds in layers of rock that they date as being older than *Archaeopteryx*. This creature was not on its way to becoming a bird—it **was** a bird!

One evolutionist has admitted: "Paleontologists have tried to turn *Archaeopteryx* into an earth-bound, feathered dinosaur. But it's not. It is a bird, a perching bird." Sadly, in spite of such admissions as this one, and in spite of all of the evidence that points to this animal simply being a bird, the *Archaeopteryx* hoax continues to be taught in science textbooks.

Animals did not slowly evolve from one kind into another. Instead, God created them separately in the Creation week (read Genesis 1-2). The Bible clearly shows that birds were birds from the beginning of their existence. They were created on day five of the Creation week. According to the Bible, birds were flying before dinosaurs were formed on the following day (Genesis 1:25).

Just because one animal looks a little like another does not mean that one evolved from the other. It simply means that God knew the design would work well in both animals. For example, since rubber tires work well for machines that have wheels, many machines with wheels have rubber tires (like airplanes, cars, and bicycles). Just because two animals have some similar features, does not mean that the animals evolved from a common ancestor. Actually, similarity between creatures (like dinosaurs and birds) is evidence of a common Designer, not a common ancestry.

The country of Bhutan featured the hoatzin on one of its mailing stamps (above). Both the hoatzin and the touraco have claws on their wings early in their lives.

Scientists are not sure how *Archaeopteryx* used its feathers. Some think that it could climb trees with its

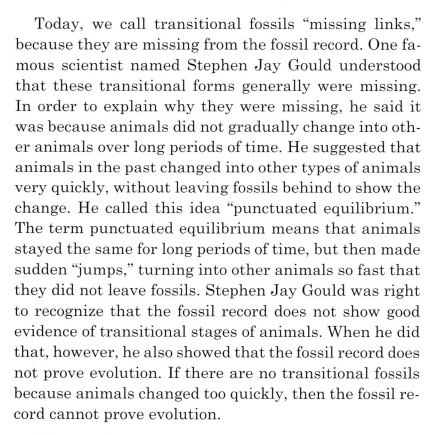

> # Archaeopteryx was not on its way to becoming a bird. It was a bird.

claws, and then simply glide to the ground with its wings. Others think that it could flap its wings, take off, and fly quite well. Since *Archaeopteryx* is extinct, we may never know for certain. We can be sure, however, that this amazing creature is **not** a missing link between dinosaurs and birds!

PUNCTUATED EQUILIBRIUM

Stephen Jay Gould

Today, we call transitional fossils "missing links," because they are missing from the fossil record. One famous scientist named Stephen Jay Gould understood that these transitional forms generally were missing. In order to explain why they were missing, he said it was because animals did not gradually change into other animals over long periods of time. He suggested that animals in the past changed into other types of animals very quickly, without leaving fossils behind to show the change. He called this idea "punctuated equilibrium." The term punctuated equilibrium means that animals stayed the same for long periods of time, but then made sudden "jumps," turning into other animals so fast that they did not leave fossils. Stephen Jay Gould was right to recognize that the fossil record does not show good evidence of transitional stages of animals. When he did that, however, he also showed that the fossil record does not prove evolution. If there are no transitional fossils because animals changed too quickly, then the fossil record cannot prove evolution.

When we look at the fossil record, we see many animals showing up very suddenly. There are no transitional fossils that build up to them. In one level of the fossil record, known as the Cambrian strata, we find thousands of animals that just "appear" without any transitional fossils to show how they supposedly evolved. This is called the "Cambrian explosion," because animals just seem to have "exploded" into the world without gradually changing from one animal to another.

As we look at this explosion of life, it is exactly what we would expect to find if animals were created and did not evolve. One evolutionist named Richard Dawkins said this about the Cambrian explosion: "The Cambrian strata of rocks...are the oldest in which we find most of the major invertebrate [animals without backbones] groups. And we find many of them already in an advanced state of evolution the very first time they appear. It is as though they were just planted there, without any evolutionary history. Needless to say, this appearance of sudden planting has delighted creationists." Why does this fact delight those who believe in creation? If God created animals, you would expect to find them fully formed, suddenly appearing in the fossil record. And that is exactly what we find.

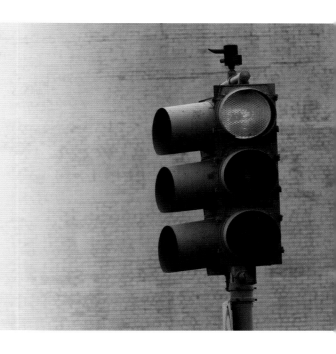

Charles Darwin thought we should find an enormous number of transitional fossils. He suggested that if those fossils were not found, that would be a major problem for his theory. After digging fossils for over 145 years, not one single transitional fossil can be proven to exist. The fossil record does not show that animals gradually changed into other animals. When we look more closely at the fossil record, we find animals exploding (suddenly appearing) fully formed, which is exactly what we should expect since God created the animals. One evolutionist, Mark Ridley, said: "In any case, no real evolutionist, whether gradualist or punctuationist, uses the fossil record as evidence in favor of the theory of evolution as opposed to special creation...." He was right. The fossil record does not prove evolution!

Richard Dawkins

UNIFORMITARIANISM

Many geologists say that things happen now just like they happened in the past—an idea known as uniformitarianism [YOU-ni-FOR-mi-TARE-ee-an-izum]. They say that "the present is the key to the past." Here is how this idea works. Suppose that you turned on your water hose in the backyard. The water from the hose begins to erode a small channel through the mud. If you measured how much mud it eroded per minute, then you could calculate how long the water had been running. For instance, if the water eroded 1 inch of mud every minute, and the channel that was cut through the mud was 20 inches deep, then according to the idea of uniformitarianism, the hose would have been on for 20 minutes. This idea works well to measure some things, but it also has numerous problems.

For instance, suppose you walk into a yard that has a 30-inch channel running through it, with water from a water hose that is eroding an inch a minute. You would probably assume the water hose had been running for 30 minutes. You decide to ask the owners of the yard, so you knock on the door. The owner of the yard informs you that firemen had just come by and used their big hose in his yard. It took them 2 minutes to erode the channel with their great big hose. He also told you that he had only been running his hose for 1 minute. You see, the problem with the idea of uniformitarianism is that many things happened in the past that are not still happening now. The Flood of Noah is a good example of an event that would have caused major miscalculations for those who try to use the idea of uniformitarianism. Let's look at some things that do not make sense if the idea of uniformitarianism is applied to them.

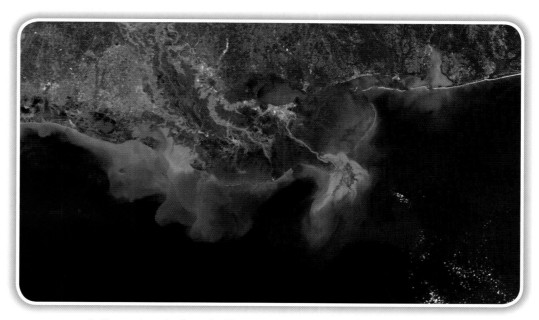

Sediment deposits from the Mississippi River delta into the Gulf of Mexico.

As the Mississippi River flows down toward the Gulf of Mexico, along the way it picks up dirt and sediment from the riverbank. Approximately 500 million tons of sediment are deposited into the Gulf of Mexico by the Mississippi River **each year**. You do the math. If the Earth really has been around as long as evolutionists say, then the sediment deposited from the Mississippi River would have filled in the Gulf of Mexico a long time ago!

Also, evolutionists believe that the Grand Canyon was formed by the Colorado River (a small amount of water) over a long period of time. The Grand Canyon is 277 miles long, 18 miles at its widest point, and 6,000 feet deep at its deepest point. If you have ever seen it in person, or seen pictures on TV or in books, then you know that it is absolutely beautiful. It has massive cliffs, huge rock formations, and a beautiful river running through the middle of it.

Evolutionists say the river (called the Colorado River) started at the bottom of the Grand Canyon and slowly, over millions of years, cut and carved that huge canyon. They say that it took a massive amount of water to form the canyon, and they do not know where else the water could have come from, except the river. Another problem with this theory is that there are over 900 cubic miles of dirt **missing** from the end of the river. Again, you do the math: If the Colorado River formed the canyon, what happened to the 900 cubic miles of dirt?

Fortunately, we have the Bible to help us out. The Bible tells about how there once was an enormous amount of water that poured down and covered the entire Earth. The Flood of Noah's day covered the Earth with water. It not only filled the valleys and plains, but also covered every mountain—even the tallest ones of Noah's day. When the Flood was over, God made the waters recede, and a lot of water was being moved around. This is the amount of water that the scientists say would have been able to carve such a huge hole. So, the Grand Canyon was not made by the river of water that is there now. Most likely, the Flood God sent upon the Earth "carved" much of what we know as the Grand Canyon.

The Flood God sent upon the Earth most likely "carved" much of what we know as the Grand Canyon.

In recent times, we have seen how a large flood can carve out a canyon like the Grand Canyon. On May 18, 1980, the Mount St. Helens volcano erupted. It was one of the most-watched volcanic eruptions of all time. Everything that scientists have learned from the 1980 eruption has yet to be measured. But certain things caused by the explosion have made geologists take a closer look at how they view the Earth.

The effects of Mount St. Helens have cast some serious doubt on the long-held uniformitarian theory that the Grand Canyon must have been slowly carved over millions of years. Before the eruption, Spirit Lake (the lake close to Mount St. Helens) drained into the Toutle River. The upper river, however, was buried by up to 600 feet of debris from the eruption, which blocked the lake's usual drainage site. For two full years, Spirit Lake was unable to drain into the Toutle River. Then, on March 19, 1982, a small eruption around the summit of Mount St. Helens caused a mudflow that was 20 miles long. The flow quickly cut a Canyon that was 140 feet deep. The canyon produced by the mudflow has been called "The Little Grand Canyon." It got its name because it appears to be a one-fortieth scale model of the Grand Canyon.

The "little Grand Canyon"

Let's think about this. If the eruption of Mount St. Helens could cause a situation in which a canyon one-fortieth the size of the Grand Canyon was formed in **one day**, then what would a person expect to happen when the "fountains of the deep" were broken up and the entire world was covered by water (as in Noah's Flood)? Surely, the evidence from Mount St. Helens shows that a huge flood could have caused the Grand Canyon.

In addition, scientists recently discovered that the island of Britain was formed by a huge flood. In fact, these scientists tell us that it was the biggest flood that any scientist has ever studied. They believe that the megaflood which caused Britain released 35 million cubic feet of water per second, which is 100 times greater than the water that the Mississippi River discharges. (A man named Thomas Wagner wrote about this flood in an article titled "Study: Flooding Left Britain an Island.") The Flood of Noah's day would have been a huge flood that could easily have caused the island of Britain.

After looking at the evidence, we can see that things have not always happened the way they happen now. The idea of uniformitarianism has several problems. One of the biggest problems is that the Flood of Noah would have caused many things (like a canyon) to form quickly. Also, polystrate fossils show that the layers of the Earth were not laid down over millions of years. The geologic column does not prove evolution. In fact, it is good evidence that points to a global flood.

Extra Evidence

➢ Even though the Mount St. Helens eruption was big, many other eruptions throughout history have been much larger.

➢ One recorded eruption in Yellowstone National Park had over 2,000 times the explosive power as the one at Mount St. Helens in May of 1980.

PANGAEA

If you look at a map of the world, it appears that many of the continents could fit together nicely—like pieces of a puzzle. Geologists in the twenty-first century largely believe that, at some time in the distant past, the continents formed a single land mass called Pangaea (PAN-gee-uh). The "continental drift" theory (now better known as the theory of plate tectonics) tries to describe how this land mass eventually broke into several separate continents and "drifted" to the positions in which we see them today. According to evolutionists, this drifting has been going on for over 250 million years.

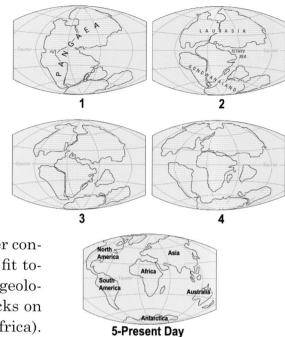

No one knows for sure if the seven continents of the Earth ever were connected. However, there does seem to be a nice fit between the continents on both sides of the Atlantic Ocean. If you place North America and South America on a map next to Europe and Africa, then "squeeze" the other continents together, it appears that they could have fit together nicely at one time in the distant past. Also, geologists have found the same kinds of fossils and rocks on neighboring continents (like South America and Africa).

5-Present Day

Although we cannot be 100% certain whether the continents once fit together and then separated, we can be sure that if they did drift apart, it did not take millions of years like evolutionists would have us believe. If land was originally a single unit, one biblical explanation for the multiple continents now present would be the Flood. The impact of a global flood would have been catastrophic, greatly reshaping and shifting the surface of the Earth. The fact that "all the fountains of the great deep were broken up" (Genesis 7:11) during the Flood could have been responsible for much continental movement.

MOUNTAIN FORMATION

Evolutionists suggest that mountains are the result of millions of years of geologic activity. Some mountains, we are told, are the result of land being "squeezed" together. Some are the result of an upward push of the Earth's crust from forces inside the Earth. Others have been caused by movement of rock along fault lines, or by volcanic activity.

The Bible reveals that **all** land was created by God during the Creation week. After creating an Earth covered by water on day one of Creation (Genesis 1:1-2), God said on day three, "let the dry land appear" (1:9). This Earth and the land that stood out from the water came into existence by the word of God, not by millions of years of evolution. Many of the hills and the valleys, were most likely created by God during the Creation week. In Psalm 104:6-8, the writer praises God for having established the heights and depths for the Earth's mountains and valleys.

> You covered it with the deep as with a garment; the waters were standing above the mountains. At Your rebuke they fled, at the sound of Your thunder they hurried away. **The mountains rose; the valleys sank down to the place which You established for them.** You set a boundary that they may not pass over, so that they will not return to cover the earth (NASB).

Both during the Creation week and during the Flood of Noah, God caused tremendous upheavals in the

Earth's crust. During the Creation week, it was caused when He made the land to appear from water. During the Flood, changes in the Earth's topography took place when "all the fountains of the great deep were broken up and the windows of heaven were opened" (Genesis 7:11), and the Earth was completely "flooded with water" (2 Peter 3:6).

According to the Bible, the mountains and valleys we see around us today are the result of God's magnificent power. He originally spoke them into existence at Creation, and later, during the Flood, caused more geologic turbulence so as to reshape them even further.

||||||||||||||||||||||||||||||||||||||||||||||||

"O God of our salvation...Who established the mountains by His strength" (Psalm 65:5-6).

||||||||||||||||||||||||||||||||||||||||||||||||

THE ICE AGE

Although the Bible does not specifically reveal the cause of the millions of cubic miles of ice on the Earth today (such as that which covers the Arctic and Antarctica), and even though the Bible does not reveal specific information about a time when ice apparently covered much of northern Europe, northwest Asia, and North America, it is likely that these ice sheets formed as a result of the Noahic Flood.

Two factors explain the build up of ice sheets: (1) increased snowfall; and (2) cooler summers. With more snowfall in the winter, and less snow melting in the summer due to cooler temperatures, snow could build up rapidly and turn into ice. But what could cause more snowfall and cooler summers? Where did the trillions of gallons of water come from that were needed to make the snow that formed the massive ice sheets? What drastic event could have changed the weather so much that this water turned into snow, and eventually into thousands of cubic miles of ice? One event comes to mind that could adequately explain such a phenomenon—the Noahic Flood.

The Flood would have changed the weather on Earth drastically. Reduced summertime temperatures could have been caused by volcanic dust (produced during the upheavals of the Flood) or by increased cloud cover that shielded the planet from some of the Sun's light. This, in turn, could have caused a rapid cooling of certain landmasses, an effect which allowed snow to remain during the summer months in certain areas of the world where it currently does not linger during the summer. Over time, this snow would compact and form huge sheets of ice that would not begin to melt away until the weather patterns on Earth changed.

While we cannot be sure about all of the causes of the Ice Age, we can offer possible explanations that would not require millions of years, and that would take into account the biblical record of the Flood.

Extra Evidence: Icicles Made of Stone

Jimmy had never been in a cave before, but his parents had promised that they could visit the Lost Sea on their next trip to Grandma's house. The Lost Sea is a huge underground body of water that is located deep in a cave in Tennessee. Jimmy was excited as they arrived at the cave.

After a few minutes in the dimly lit cavern, Jimmy's eyes adjusted to the darkness and he could see strange things hanging from the ceiling. Similar things looked like they were growing from the floor of the cave as well. They looked like huge icicles, but they appeared to be made out of rock. "What are those things?" Jimmy asked his dad. "The ones hanging from the ceiling are called stalactites, and the ones attached to the floor are stalagmites," replied Jimmy's dad.

"How did they form?" asked Jimmy. His dad explained that water above the caves seeps through the ground. As it does, a mineral called calcium carbonate gets mixed in with the water. Eventually, the mineral-filled water seeps through the sides or ceiling of a cavern. This water forms little drops that evaporate, leaving behind the calcium carbonate. Sometimes, the water droplets fall to the floor of the cave and still have some minerals left in them. When this happens, a stalagmite often "builds up" from the floor.

"That must take a long time," said Jimmy as he thought out loud. "Many people used to think so," replied his dad. "But scientists have discovered that it does not take that

➪

long. In fact, some stalactites have grown as big as five feet in only forty-five years. They grow especially quickly in tropical areas where it rains a lot and the rainwater seeps through the ground. Stalactites and stalagmites that once were thought to have taken more than 10,000 years to grow could have grown in just a few hundred."

Many who believe in evolution claim that stalactites and stalagmites grow very slowly. They suggest that it would have taken thousands, or even millions of years for certain stalactites to form. This is not true. Today, we know that they can form very quickly. In fact, one stalagmite found in the Carlsbad Caverns in New Mexico (and pictured in *National Geographic* magazine) had a bat preserved in it. The dead bat had fallen on the stalagmite, and before it had time to decay, the stalagmite had grown over it.

In addition, stalactites often form on manmade structures that are known to be only a few years old. In Washington D.C. on the Lincoln Memorial, a picture from 1968 shows that stalactites had grown to be over five feet long in just 45 years since the monument was built in 1923. One tunnel in Raccoon Mountain, near Chattanooga, Tennessee, was blasted out of the rock in 1977. In the few years since it was created, stalactites have formed. Also, several other manmade bridges and tunnels, especially in Philadelphia, Pennsylvania, have stalactites hanging from them. Stalactites do not take millions, or even thousands of years to form.

Even though some stalactites are forming fairly slowly today, that does not mean that they always formed slowly. Since we know they can form very quickly, then it is a possibility that they formed quickly in the past. Simply put, stalactites and stalagmites do not prove that the Earth is old.

CHAPTER REVIEW

FILL IN THE BLANKS

1. The idea that things happen now just like they happened in the past is known as _____.

2. Layers of the Earth are collectively known as the _____ _____.

3. The _____ _____ is the time in history when glaciers covered northern Europe, northwest Asia, and North America.

4. _____ is the study of the Earth.

5. The effects of _____ _____ account for mountains, canyons, and many other geologic formations.

6. The law of _____ is the evolutionary belief that the layers on the bottom of the geologic column are the oldest layers, while the layers on the top are the youngest layers.

7. Many 21st century geologists believe that the continents once formed a single land mass called _____.

8. The _____ _____ theory suggests that over 250 million years, the landmasses of Pangaea separated.

TRUE/FALSE

1. ____ The Earth is 4.6 billion years old.

2. ____ Diatoms are gold minerals.

3. ____ The global Flood of Noah could account for the formation of mountains and canyons.

4. ____ The geologic column gives good evidence for the evolution of species.

5. ____ Polystrate animal fossils have been discovered by geologists.

6. ____ There are less than 200 cubic miles of dirt missing from the end of the Colorado River.

7. ____ Many 21st century geologists believe that at some time in the distant past, the continents formed a single land mass called Pangaea.

8. ____ We can be 100% sure that the continents once fit together and then separated.

9. ____ Noah's Flood could explain the rising of some mountain ranges.

SHORT ANSWER

1. Briefly explain why the trilobite is evidence of Creation.

2. How do evolutionary scientists propose that the Grand Canyon was formed?

3. How do creation scientists explain the formation of the Grand Canyon?

4. What two factors logically explain the build up of ice sheets?

5. Resulting mud flow from what volcano caused the formation of "The Little Grand Canyon."

6. How many feet deep is the Grand Canyon?

MULTIPLE CHOICE

1. The law of superposition says that the layers on the bottom of the geologic column are the _____ layers, while the top layers are the _____ layers.
   A. Newest, Oldest
   B. Oldest, Youngest
   C. Solid, Gaseous
   D. Liquid, Solid

2. "Polystrate" means _____.
   A. Many layers
   B. Around the Earth
   C. Slightly curved
   D. Few cells

3. In 1976, geologists discovered a whale fossil covered with diatoms, which are _____.
   A. Gold minerals
   B. Fern-like plants
   C. Hydrogen particles
   D. Microscopic algae

4. Evolutionists claim that the Earth is _____ years old.
   A. 3.7 thousand
   B. 6 thousand
   C. 4.6 billion
   D. 23 million

5. The geologic column does not prove evolution; rather it is good evidence that points to a(n) _____.
   A. Meteor crash
   B. Global flood
   C. Global earthquake
   D. Implosion of the Earth

6. _____ is another name for the continental drift theory.
   A. Pangaea Theory
   B. Theory of Topography
   C. Theory of Superfluity
   D. Theory of Plate Tectonics.

7. Though it is located toward the bottom of the geologic column, the eye of the _____ is more complex than that of any creature, past or present.
   A. Trilobite
   B. Bumblebee
   C. *Stegosaurus*
   D. Hummingbird

8. Which of these gives evidence of a global flood?
   A. Polystrate fossils
   B. Ice Age
   C. Mountain formation
   D. All of the above

9. The Grand Canyon is _____ wide at its widest point.
   A. 898 feet
   B. 277 yards
   C. 18 miles
   D. 54 miles

10. The Mississippi River deposits _____ of sediment into the Gulf of Mexico each year.
    A. 2,000 square inches
    B. 100 cubic feet
    C. 3,000 cubic yards
    D. 500 million tons

11. The geologic column gives good evidence for the evolution of _____.
    A. Trees
    B. Whales
    C. Trilobites
    D. Nothing

CHAPTER–6
THE AGE OF THE EARTH

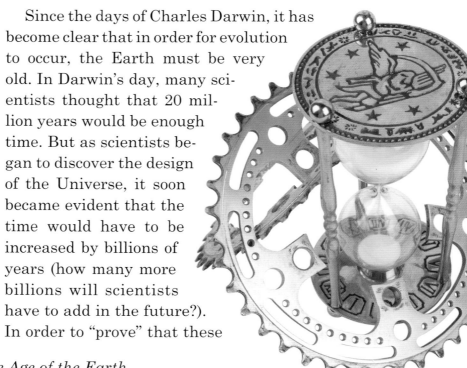

ost of you don't use words or phrases like half-life, radiometric, and daughter element in everyday conversation. In fact, you are probably much more interested in PE class than you are in studying the methods used to date the Earth. However, since most science books and school textbooks are selling you a lie by telling you that the Earth can be dated at almost 5 billion years old (and the Universe at almost 14 billion), you deserve to hear the truth.

But, before we start this study on dating methods, you have the right to ask a very valid question: "Why does the age of the Earth matter?" The answer is simple. The Bible presents evidence to establish that the Earth is only a few thousand years old. Most scientists suggest that it is billions of years old. If the dating methods these scientists use are right, then the Bible is wrong. However, if the dating methods that give billions of years are wrong, then the Bible remains the inspired Word of God that can be trusted.

Since the days of Charles Darwin, it has become clear that in order for evolution to occur, the Earth must be very old. In Darwin's day, many scientists thought that 20 million years would be enough time. But as scientists began to discover the design of the Universe, it soon became evident that the time would have to be increased by billions of years (how many more billions will scientists have to add in the future?). In order to "prove" that these billions of years actually occurred, certain dating methods have been invented to calculate the Earth's age. If you have taken Earth science in school, then you have studied the different ways that scientists "date" the rocks and other materials of the Earth. The goal of this chapter is to show (without going into technical details) that the dating methods yielding billions of years have some serious flaws in them.

Charles Darwin

PROBLEMS WITH RADIOMETRIC DATING

New ways of dating rocks are supposed to be able to give ages in the billions of years. These are the radiometric dating methods. Each of these methods is based upon the decay rate of certain elements. In one method, for instance, the element uranium-238 will break down into the element lead over a period of many years. The element that breaks down (in this case, uranium-238) is called the parent element. The element that is formed (in this case, lead) is called the daughter element. How long is this supposed to take? In the case of uranium and lead, the half-life is supposed to be 4.5 billion years. A half-life is simply the time that it takes half of a sample of the parent element to turn into the daughter element. For instance, if you have 50 ounces of uranium, then in 4.5 billion years you supposedly should have 25 ounces of uranium and about that many ounces of lead. Therefore, if you know the rate of decay for an element, once you measure the amount of the two elements in the rock sample, simple math should give you an age for the rock. However, there are certain things that scientists must assume in order for radiometric dating to work. Let's look at those assumptions.

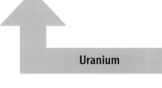

Uranium

Lead

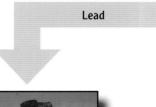

ASSUMPTION 1: THE RATE OF DECAY HAS ALWAYS BEEN THE SAME

The first major assumption built into radiometric dating is the idea that the parent elements have decayed in the past at the exact same rate as they are decaying today. This idea has problems, because no one alive today knows what kind of environment existed in the distant past. We cannot claim to know how fast elements decayed in the past, because we have very little evidence to prove this idea (which is why it is an assumption). Let's consider how badly this idea could alter the age of the Earth. Suppose you come upon a man who is cutting down trees in a forest. You watch him for an entire hour, and he cuts down only 1 tree. Then you count the number of trees he has cut—31 in all. If you assume that he has been cutting trees down at the same rate all day, then you calculate that he has chopped for 31 hours. However, when you talk to the man, he tells you that, earlier in the day when his ax was sharp and his stomach was full, he was cutting down 5 trees an hour; only

in the last hour had he slacked off. With this information, you now understand that he worked for only 7 hours, not 31. Claiming that the decay rates in the past were the same as they are now is an assumption that cannot be proven and should not be granted to those who want an age for the Earth measured in billions of years.

ASSUMPTION 2: ELEMENTS HAVE NOT BEEN AFFECTED BY OUTSIDE FORCES

Another assumption built into the radiometric dating methods is the idea that the elements have not been affected by outside forces. This means that no water has soaked through the sample and "carried away" some of the lead, or that none of the uranium had a chance to escape through holes in the rock. But how can a person claim that natural forces have not affected the elements in a rock for a period of billions of years? In 4.5 billion years, could it be slightly possible that water seeped through the sample and added or subtracted some lead or uranium? Furthermore, could there be an "outside chance" that some of the uranium seeped out of pores in the rock? If any rock were really 4.5 billion years old, no one in this world would have a clue what had or had not gone in or out of the rock over that vast amount of time. Once again, the assumption that certain rock samples are "closed systems" simply cannot be granted.

But how can a person claim that natural forces have not affected the elements in a rock for a period of billions of years?

ASSUMPTION 3: NO DAUGHTER ELEMENT EXISTED AT THE BEGINNING

To date rocks using any radiometric dating system, a person must assume that the daughter element in the sample was not there in the beginning. However, that claim cannot be proven. Who is to say that the rock did not start out with 23 ounces of lead already in it? The lead could have been in the rock from the beginning (and so could the uranium). To illustrate this point, suppose you go to a swimming pool and find a hose that is pumping water into the pool at a rate of 100 gallons an hour. You discover that the pool has 3,000 gallons of water in it. You calculate that the hose must have been running for 30 hours. However, when you ask the owner of the pool how long she has been running the hose, she tells you that she has been running it for only 1 hour. Most of the water was already in the pool due to a heavy rain the night before. If you assumed that all the water came from the hose, your calculations would be way off—29 hours off to be exact. Assumption three—that no daughter element existed at the beginning—simply cannot be granted.

ANOTHER PROBLEM WITH RADIOMETRIC DATING

In addition to the assumptions that are built into radiometric dating, another problem is that the different radiometric methods drastically disagree with one another at times. On occasion, the same sample of rock can be dated by the different methods, and the dates can differ by several hundred million years. Some rocks from Hawaii that were known to have formed about two hundred years ago rendered a date of 160 million to 3 billion years when dated by the potassium-argon method. Another time, the same basalt rock in Nigeria was given a date of 95 million years when dated by the potassium-argon method, and 750 million years when dated by the uranium-helium method. But what can you expect from dating methods that are based entirely on built-in assumptions? Anything is possible!

It is likely that other dating methods soon will be "discovered" that will give even older ages for the Earth. But each dating method that renders colossal numbers of years will be based on similar, unprovable assumptions. All around you, books, television, and radio are telling you that the Earth is billions of years old. This is nothing more than a trick to discredit the real history of the Earth as found in the Bible. Realizing that these vast ages of billions of years come from dating methods that are based upon incorrect assumptions will give you more confidence in the Bible. There never have been billions of years available for evolution.

Basalt

LIMITATIONS OF RADIOCARBON DATING

Another dating method often discussed when studying one of the various sciences is radiocarbon dating (also known as carbon-14 dating). Some people who defend the theory of evolution have been known to say that this method of dating supports the idea that the Earth is billions of years old. The truth is, however, carbon-14 dating is totally ineffective in measuring the millions (or billions) of years needed by evolutionists. Many people do not understand that carbon-14 dating can be used to date only organic material (things that were once living—such as plants, animals, and hu-

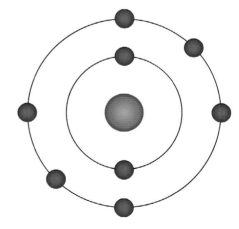

Carbon Atom

> ## Radiocarbon dating "is no good for the evolutionary timescale where we are dealing in millions of years."

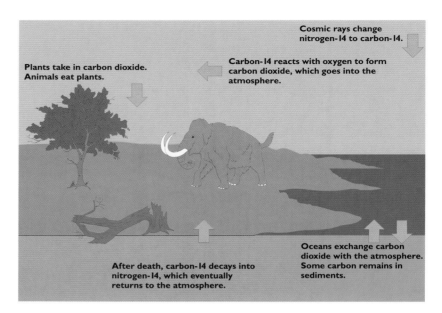

Plants take in carbon dioxide. Animals eat plants.

Cosmic rays change nitrogen-14 to carbon-14.

Carbon-14 reacts with oxygen to form carbon dioxide, which goes into the atmosphere.

After death, carbon-14 decays into nitrogen-14, which eventually returns to the atmosphere.

Oceans exchange carbon dioxide with the atmosphere. Some carbon remains in sediments.

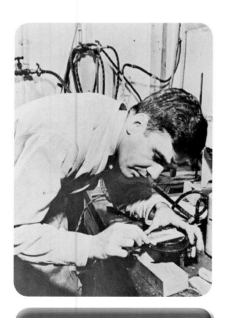

In 1940, Martin Kamen (pictured above) and Samuel Ruben discovered carbon-14. That discovery enabled Willard Libby of UC Berkeley to invent radiocarbon dating in 1949.

mans), or that it can be used only to date things that are relatively young.

Evolutionist Richard Dawkins acknowledged the weakness of radiocarbon dating when he said, "It is useful for dating organic material where we are dealing in hundreds or a few thousands of years, but it is no good for the evolutionary timescale where we are dealing in millions of years." Even the inventor of carbon-14 dating, W.F. Libby, acknowledged that it could not be used to get accurate ages measured in millions or billions of years.

In addition, carbon-14 dating has been shown to be far from perfect in measuring organic material. Wood taken from actively growing trees has been dated by this method as being 10,000 years old. Also, when scientists tested two parts of a frozen musk ox found in Fairbanks, Alaska, two vastly different dates were given. Radiocarbon testing falsely showed that one part of the musk ox was 24,000 years old, while another part was only 7,200 years old.

Obviously, carbon-14 dating cannot accurately render dates for the age of the Earth in billions of years. It has trouble even with items measured in hundreds or thousands of years.

DOESN'T THE EARTH LOOK OLD?

There are many people who think the Earth looks very old. To them it looks to be very worn in places—like it's been around for a few billion years. But what does a young Earth actually look like? And does an old "looking" Earth mean God didn't create this Earth? The doctrine of apparent age suggests that the things God made during the Creation week were formed complete

and fully functional. For instance, how old was Adam five seconds after God created him? He was five seconds old! Yet he walked, communicated with God, and looked like an adult human being. In fact we learn that God gave Adam and Eve plants that bore seeds and fruits from trees before He rested on day seven. So if a tree were cut down in the Garden of Eden on day seven, how many rings would it have had? Possibly hundreds, yet it would

Questions to Consider

◇ How old do you think Adam looked the day after his creation?

◇ How effective would tree-ring dating have been by the end of the Creation week?

have been only four days old (since plants were made on day three of Creation). So, the **real** age of the tree and the **apparent** age of the tree would have been many years apart. Just because some things about the Earth may "appear" older than a few thousand years, does not mean they are that old.

HOW COAL FORMS

According to scientists who believe in evolution, coal formed millions of years ago. Supposedly, in swamps and bogs, plants began to die and fall to the bottom of the swamp. Over many years, these plants were buried by other dead plants, and formed a substance known as peat. Eventually, the decomposing plants, due to heat, pressure, and weight on them, turned from peat into coal. The plants that died and formed into coal are supposed to be millions of years old. And evolutionists teach that it took millions of years for coal to form.

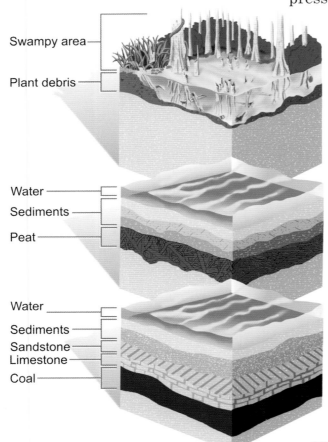

Swampy area

Plant debris

Water

Sediments

Peat

Water

Sediments

Sandstone

Limestone

Coal

We know today that it does not take millions of years for coal to form. In fact, there is nowhere on Earth that coal is forming slowly in swamps or bogs. We have learned that coal did not form millions of years ago. And we now know that coal can form in just a few years. Let's look at some evidence.

It is true that coal is made out of dead plants. These plants, however, did not fall into swamps and build up over millions of years. In fact, from what we know about coal, many of these plants died and were buried very quickly. For example, when we look into coal, we often find tree trunks standing upright going through many layers. If the coal formed over millions of years, the tree trunks would have fallen and decomposed. What could have killed many plants all at once, and then buried them quickly? The Flood of Noah would be a great way to explain much of the coal on the Earth.

According to the Bible, the Great Flood happened only a few thousand years ago. That would not have been enough time for coal to form, would it? Actually, coal does not take millions, or even thousands of years, to form. Coal can be formed very quickly. In order for coal to form, dead plants must be buried. Then, the plants must be put under pressure and heated. In science laboratories, scientists have proven that coal can form in only a few months. It is not necessary to have millions or even thousands of years to form coal. For instance, near Frieburg, Germany, an old wooden bridge was being replaced with a metal structure. The wooden pillars of the bridge had been in the ground only about a hundred years. Yet, when the bases were pulled out of the ground, they had already partially turned to coal. Under the right conditions, coal can form in a few months or years. The Flood of Noah's day would have buried thousands of tons of plants and animals very quickly. The heat and pressure of this burial could have easily formed the huge coal beds we see today.

In a laboratory, coal can be produced by machines in only a few months. If the right conditions are present in nature, coal can be formed in a short time as well.

We also can prove that many of the things we find in coal are not millions of years old like many people teach. As an example, according to evolutionists, the coal in the Upper Carboniferous layer is supposed to be 250 million years old. Humans did not evolve, according to this theory, until about 3 million years ago. Yet, we have found human footprints in coal layers that are supposed to be 250 million years old. How could the coal layers be 250 million years old, if the humans who made tracks in them did not evolve until 247 million years after the coal formed? The truth is, neither humans nor coal are millions of years old. After the Flood, Noah or his descendants could have left their footprints in the coal while it was just beginning to form a few thousand years ago.

Coal

In summary, coal forms when plants are buried very quickly. The upright trees in coal prove this. Scientists are now able to form coal in laboratories in only a few months, so we know it does not take millions of years to form. Furthermore, things like human footprints show that coal is not millions of years old.

EVIDENCE FOR A YOUNG EARTH

THE EARTH'S DECAYING MAGNETIC FIELD

If you go hiking or camping, you might take along a compass to make sure that you do not get lost. When you look at the compass, you see that the arrow of the compass always points to the north; it never points to the south or west (unless your compass is broken). Have you ever wondered why compasses point north?

The answer has to do with the Earth's magnetic field. In the core of the Earth, a huge electric current is produced that causes the Earth to produce a magnetic attraction. That magnetic attraction is what causes the arrow on your compass to point North. What does this have to do with the Earth's age? Scientists who have been studying the Earth's magnetic forces have discovered that those forces are getting weaker and weaker every year. One government report stated that the magnetic field would be gone by the year A.D. 3991.

If we look at how fast the magnetic field is decaying today, and try to calculate how long it has been decaying, we learn something very interesting. If you go backward for just a few thousand years, the heat inside the Earth would have been so great that the Earth would have broken apart and cracked. One scientist,

Thomas G. Barnes, indicated that, after measuring the magnetic field, the Earth could be only about 10,000 years old. Maybe the Earth's magnetic field did not decay in the past like it is decaying today. But, if we look at how it is decaying today, like evolutionists do with other dating methods, we get a very young Earth that is only a few thousand years old.

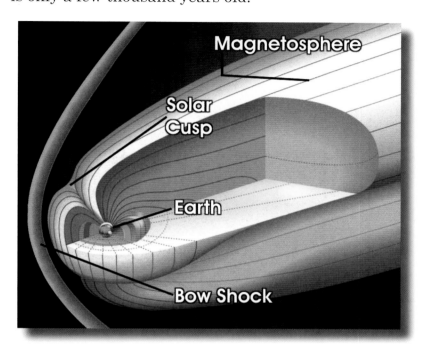

If we look at how the Earth's magnetic field is decaying today (like evolutionists do with other dating methods), we get an Earth that is only a few thousand years old.

HYDROGEN IN THE UNIVERSE

Our Universe is made up mostly of an element called hydrogen. In nature, however, hydrogen is converted into another element known as helium. It does not turn back into hydrogen once it changes. And, we have not found any way that hydrogen can be produced in large amounts. If the Universe were millions or billions of years old, then all the hydrogen would long ago have changed into helium. But that is not what we find. The Universe still contains huge amounts of hydrogen. One famous astronomer by the name of Fred Hoyle saw this as a real problem. After studying it for some time, he concluded that the idea of an old age for the Universe

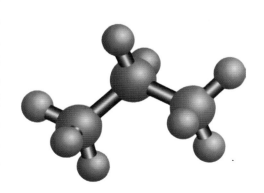

had some problems. He even thought that this piece of evidence, along with others, might point to a Creator. He was right. If the Universe has been around for billions of years, all the hydrogen would have changed into helium. But when we look at the Universe, we still see enormous amounts of hydrogen, which shows that the Universe cannot be billions of years old.

POPULATION STATISTICS

One of the strongest arguments for a young Earth comes from the field of human population statistics. According to historical records, the human population on Earth doubles approximately every 35 years. If you break down that figure, it represents an annual increase of 20,000 people per every million. Let's suppose that humankind started with just two individuals (we will call them Adam and Eve for the sake of our argument). And suppose that they lived on the Earth 1 million years ago (some evolutionists suggest that man, in one form or another, has been on the Earth 2-3 million years). Suppose, further, that an average generation (the span of time between the birth of parents and that of their children) was 42 years, and that each family had an average of 2.4 children. (They probably had many more than that, but we will use a conservative estimate that would allow for at least some population growth; if a family unit had only two children, there would be zero population growth, since each parent simply would replace himself or herself, providing no net increase.)

Allowing for wars, famine, diseases, and other devastation, there would be approximately 1×10^{5000} people on the Earth today! That number is a 1 followed by 5,000

zeroes. But the entire Universe (at an estimated size of 20 billion light-years in diameter) would hold only 1×10^{100} people. However, using young-Earth figures (of eight people having survived the Noahic Flood), the current world population would be around 5-6 billion people. The question is—which of the two figures is almost right on target, and which could not possibly be correct? Henry Morris and his son John wrote about this in their book *Science & Creation*.

THE BIBLE AND THE AGE OF THE EARTH

Have you ever heard people talk about their family tree? A family tree basically is a diagram of someone's family history. It includes the names of parents, grandparents, great grandparents, and so on. Many times, people are able to find out a lot of interesting information about their ancestors by reading their family tree. They can learn their ancestors' full names, when they were born, when they were married, and possibly when they died. This information is helpful, not only in determining who their ancestors were, but also in showing how long ago they lived.

Similar to these "family trees," the Bible contains lists of people (known as genealogies) who lived upon the Earth long ago. Because Jesus is the main focus of the Bible, most of the genealogies (in one way or another) revolve around Him. In fact, the Bible contains genealogies that extend from Jesus all the way back to Adam. These lists are found in such places as Genesis 5 and 11, Matthew 1, and Luke 3. The genealogy of Jesus is important because it shows that Jesus is Who He claimed to be (and Who the prophets foretold He would be)—a descendant of both Abraham and King David.

Adam

Seth

Enosh

Cainan

Mahalalel

Jared

Enoch

Methuselah

Lamech

Noah

Shem

So what does all of this have to do with the age of the Earth? Similar to figuring out how long ago your great-great-great grandfather lived by looking at your family tree, it is possible to read all of the Bible genealogies and figure out that the first man, Adam, lived on the Earth only a few thousand years ago. The reason we can associate Adam with the age of the Earth is because God told us through Moses: "For in six days the Lord made the heavens and earth, the sea, and all that is in them, and rested the seventh day" (Exodus 20:11). That means if the Earth was created on day one, and Adam was created on day six, then the Earth is only five days older than man. In addition, Jesus Himself said that "from the beginning of the creation, God made them male and female." The lengthy Bible genealogies that extend from Jesus back to Adam show that the Earth is only a few thousand years old, not millions or billions of years old, as some would have us believe.

While it is true that there is no single passage (or group of passages) in the Bible that states exactly how old the Earth is, that does not mean that we cannot calculate an approximate age for the Earth. Consider the following.

First, both world history and the Bible reveal that from the present time back to the time of Jesus was about 2,000 years. Even people who do not believe in God, and who do not believe that Jesus Christ is His Son, agree with this point. They may not accept Jesus as God's Son, but they do understand that a man named Jesus really did live in the first century. Since all time is dated from His birth, it's pretty difficult to deny His existence.

Second, from Jesus back to Abraham was about 2,000 years. This figure is available from biblical chronology. In addition, archaeologists have documented time and again that the period between the time of Abraham and the time of Jesus was about 2,000 years. And even people who do not believe in God, or accept the Bible as His Word, admit that this is true.

> ## "For in six days the Lord made the heavens and earth, the sea, and all that is in them, and rested the seventh day"
> **(Exodus 20:11).**

That leaves just one last section of time—the period from Abraham back to Adam. Moses (Genesis 1) and Paul (1 Corinthians 15:45) both recorded that Adam was the first man to live upon the Earth. And we know from Genesis 1 and Exodus 20:11 that the Earth was created on day one, while man was created on day six. So, if we could determine the length of time between Abraham and Adam, we would be within five days of the age of the Earth. Can we do that? Yes, we can.

In some of the genealogies listed in the Bible (like in Genesis 5), the age of the father at the time his son was born is provided. Using that information, it is possible to obtain an estimate of how much time would have passed between Abraham and Adam. As it turns out, that period was roughly 2,000 years.

Added together, these three numbers equal about 6,000 years. It may be that a few hundred years could be added within the genealogies, but it is impossible for millions of years to fit in them. Just as you can know that your great-great-great...grandpa did not live 10 million years ago, we can know for sure by consulting the biblical genealogies that the Earth is not millions or billions of years old, but only a few thousand years old.

CHAPTER REVIEW

FILL IN THE BLANKS

1. When given the right conditions, _____ can be created within a matter of weeks, or even days.

2. The Universe is made up, in large part, of a gas called _____, and is converted, over time, into another gas known as _____.

3. _____ was the first man to exist on the Earth.

4. If the Earth is billions of years old, then the population on Earth would be around _____ people.

5. A huge electric current is produced in the Earth, called the _____ _____. After measuring this current by conventional dating methods, the Earth was measured to be only around 10,000 years old.

6. _____ is an important verse that tells us of how God created everything in six days, and then rested on the seventh day.

7. Even some well-known evolutionists have admitted that _____ dating is insufficient for measuring anything that is more than a few thousand years old.

8. The _____ is the time that it takes for one half of a parent element to change into a daughter element.

TRUE/FALSE

1. ____ Radiometric dating is not based on any unproven assumptions.

2. ____ The age of the Earth has nothing to do with the Bible.

3. ____ The different radiometric dating methods always agree.

4. ____ A one-day-old tree in Eden may have looked hundreds of years old.

5. ____ Under the right conditions, coal can form in a few weeks or months.

6. ____ It takes millions of years for coal to form.

7. ____ Human footprints have been found in coal that evolutionists date to be 250 million years old.

8. ____ Several dating methods point toward a young Earth that is only a few thousand years old.

9. ____ If the Universe has been around for billions of years, all the hydrogen would have changed into helium.

10. ____ The genealogies in the Bible point to an age for the Earth of only a few thousand years.

SHORT ANSWER

1. Name three assumptions that are made by scientists when referring to radiometric dating.

2. Why is the age of the Earth an important topic to study?

3. Give a short explanation of how radiometric dating is supposed to work.

1. What daughter element is a product of the decay of the parent element uranium-238?

   A. Carbon

   B. Aluminum

   C. Lead

   D. Thallium

2. This element is converted into helium in nature

   A. Hydrogen

   B. Calcium carbonate

   C. Limestone

   D. Coal

3. An assumption is something that has not been

   A. Written down

   B. Proven

   C. Studied

   D. None of the above

4. The idea that God created things in a mature state is known as

   A. Apparent vision

   B. Apparent delusion

   C. Apparent evolution

   D. Apparent age

5. The Bible uses these to establish an approximate age of the Earth

   A. Poems

   B. Laws

   C. Genealogies

   D. All of the above

6. This causes the arrow in a compass to point north

   A. Earth's gravitational pull

   B. Earth's magnetic field

   C. Earth's density

   D. Solar gravity

7. This man invented radiocarbon dating

   A. W.F. Libby

   B. Richard Dawkins

   C. Adam

   D. Stephen J. Gould

8. Coal is formed from a substance called

   A. Slyver

   B. Bog

   C. Peat

   D. Marsh slush

9. An astronomer who studied hydrogen and helium

   A. Kepler

   B. Isaac Newton

   C. Stephen Johnson

   D. Fred Hoyle

10. Number of people the Universe probably could hold

    A. 10^3

    B. 10^{400}

    C. 10^{100}

    D. 10^{5000}

11. Which of the following is an assumption used in radiometric dating

    A. The rate of decay has always been the same

    B. Nothing has contaminated the sample

    C. No daughter element was in the sample originally

    D. All of the above

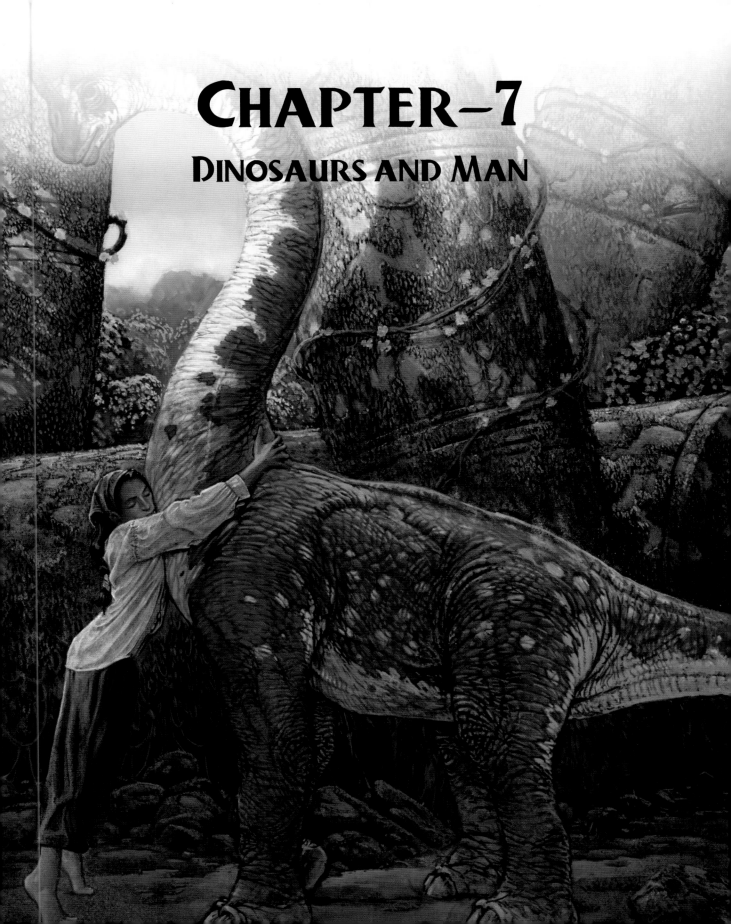

CHAPTER–7
DINOSAURS AND MAN

EVIDENCE THAT HUMANS LIVED WITH DINOSAURS

Most of us have been taught that humans did not live with dinosaurs. In fact, most science books tell us that dinosaurs lived millions of years before humans ever arrived on Earth. That simply is not true. In fact, there is much evidence which shows that humans, dinosaurs, and other extinct animals lived together only a few thousand years ago, not millions of years ago.

A Dinosaur Carved in Stone

Suppose your teacher asked you to take out a pencil and paper and draw a Kabolib. What would you draw? You probably wouldn't draw anything because you don't know what a Kabolib is and you certainly don't know what one looks like. The truth is, there is no Kabolib; it is a made-up word that has no meaning. But we can learn from this word that in order to draw something a person must see it or have it described.

In the country of Cambodia, an ancient emperor named Jayavarman VII built a temple to honor his mother. He finished building the temple in A.D. 1186. Beautiful stone statues and carvings decorate the walls and columns of the temple. In the middle of all these beautiful carvings, there is a row of animals carved on a pillar. Most of the animals are not unusual—a monkey, a deer, some parrots. But one of the animals is very interesting because it looks like a *Stegosaurus!*

Why is a carving of a *Stegosaurus* so interesting? Evolutionary scientists say that dinosaurs died out about 65 million years ago. They say that humans could not have seen real, live dinosaurs. But the carving on the Cambodian temple proves that idea is false. How would the person carving the temple almost a thousand years ago have known what a *Stegosaurus* looked like unless he had seen one, or someone had described it to him?

Today we know what dinosaurs looked like because people spend millions of dollars digging up their bones. But this digging did not start in modern times until about 1822, more than 600 years after the temple was built. The very best explanation is that whoever carved the temple had seen a *Stegosaurus*. That idea might sound strange to a person who believes in evolution, but not to someone who has read the Bible. The Bible says that God made everything in six days. He made humans on day six, along with all land-living animals. Since dinosaurs were land-living animals, they were made on day six of Creation, along with humans. The fact that humans saw dinosaurs fits perfectly with what the Bible says.

|||||||||||||||||||||||||||||||||||||||||||||

The Bible says that God made everything in six days.

|||||||||||||||||||||||||||||||||||||||||||||

NATURAL BRIDGES NATIONAL MONUMENT

Natural Bridges National Monument is located in a barren part of southeastern Utah. On the underside of its second largest bridge (Kachina Bridge), several petroglyphs (rock carvings) and pictographs (rock paintings) exist, which rock-art experts believe to be anywhere from 500 to 1,500 years old. The carvings are thought to be the work of the Anasazi Indians who once lived in that area of southeastern Utah. A mountain goat, a human figure, multiple hand prints, and many other carvings and drawings are seen easily underneath the bridge on both sides of the span. The most fascinating piece of rock art at Kachina Bridge, however, is the

To help you see the image, we have enhanced the color of certain portions and circled both the human figure in the upper left-hand section and the dinosaur figure to the right.

petroglyph that looks exactly like a dinosaur. This figure, which is carved into the rock, has a long, thick tail, a long neck, a wide midsection, and a small head. Any unbiased visitor to Kachina Bridge would have to admit that this particular petroglyph looks like a dinosaur—specifically an *Apatosaurus* (more popularly known as *Brontosaurus*). But is it really genuine? Two well-known rock-art experts have written about this particular petroglyph, and neither has suggested that it is a modern-day fake. One of these rock-art experts is a man named Francis Barnes—an evolutionist who is widely known for his knowledge on rock art of the American Southwest. He stated: "There is a petroglyph in Natural Bridges National Monument that bears a startling resemblance to a dinosaur, specifically a *Brontosaurus*, with long tail and neck, small head and all." The other evolutionary rock-art specialist, Dennis Slifer, made this statement about the same petroglyph: "One of the most curious designs is a petroglyph that resembles a dinosaur."

Truly, the dinosaur petroglyph at Natural Bridges National Monument shows every sign of being an actual drawing of a real dinosaur by a people who lived in that area of Utah hundreds, or perhaps even 1,000 years before the first dinosaur fossil was found in modern times

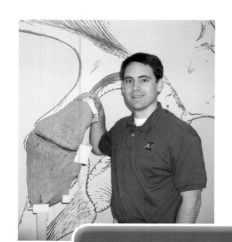

About 45 miles from the dinosaur petroglyph, The Dinosaur Museum in Blanding, Utah has a section of an *Apatosaurus* hip fossil on display that was found near the area. This find shows that the dinosaur was in the area, and could have been seen by early Indians.

(1820s). The best way to explain this drawing is to admit that people have seen dinosaurs in the past. Interestingly, about 45 miles away from the carving, bones of an *Apatosaurus* were discovered, and currently are on display at The Dinosaur Museum in Blanding, Utah.

SAMUEL HUBBARD AND THE ROCK DRAWING

In 1924, a man named Samuel Hubbard went to a place near the Grand Canyon searching for Indian artifacts. He went to the Havai Supai Canyon and began looking for old Indian relics. When he arrived, he found exactly what he was looking for. On one canyon wall he found a drawing made by the Indians many years before. The Indians had drawn a wild goat, an elephant, and a creature that looked just like—a dinosaur. Also, Dr. Hubbard and his coworkers found several fossilized dinosaur footprints within several miles of the drawing.

This picture shows the carving that Samuel Hubbard and his men discovered.

Members of Samuel Hubbard's team taking pictures at the Grand Canyon

DINOSAUR FIGURINES IN MEXICO

In 1944, a German businessman by the name of Waldemar Julsrud was riding a horse near the foot of the El Toro mountains in Acambaro, Mexico. Looking at the ground, he noticed some carved stones and ceramic pieces sticking up, half buried in the dirt. He jumped off his horse and began to dig up the artifacts, which were unlike any he had ever seen. Thinking that there might be more of the ceramics and stone carvings, he made a deal with a local farmer. For every unbroken piece the farmer dug up, Julsrud would pay him 1 peso (about 12 cents). In all, about 30,000 artifacts were found. Many of them were faces of people, musical instruments, masks, idols, and other such things. Each one was different from the others, since they were not made using a mold, but were handcrafted. Among the figurines, hundreds of dinosaur sculptures were found. Some of the dinosaur sculptures were as much as five feet long. Among the different dinosaur figurines found, dinosaurs such as the *Triceratops*, *Stegosaurus*, *Iguanodon*, *Brachiosaurus*, and *Tyrannosaurus rex* could be identified.

How could the ancient people at Acambaro have known what dinosaurs looked like if they had not seen them, or talked to people who had seen them? The truth is, dinosaurs and man have lived together in the past. God created all the animals, and Adam and Eve, on days five and six of the Creation week.

ICA BURIAL STONES

Javier Cabrera Darquea came into possession of his first burial stone (from the Ica section of the country of Peru) when he was given one as a paperweight for his birthday. Dr. Cabrera tried to find the origin of his unique gift, and eventually gathered over 11,000 of the stones. The rocks turned out to be ancient burial stones that the Indians had placed with their dead. Amazingly, almost one-third of the stones depicted specific types of dinosaurs (such as *Triceratops* and

Stegosaurus) and various pterosaurs. The type of art form represented by these stones, and their location, dated them around A.D. 500-1500, which is hundreds of years before humans began learning about dinosaurs in modern times (in the 1820s). Also of interest is the fact that several *Diplodocus*-like dinosaurs on the stones have what appear to be dermal frills (spines)—something never previously reported by scientists. Even though the Ica stones

revealed carvings of long-neck dinosaurs with spines down their neck, back, and tail long before the 1990s, it was not until 1992 that scientists first discovered dermal frills on the fossilized remains of large plant-eating dinosaurs. Regarding the sauropod dermal spines found in the Howe dinosaur quarry in Wyoming in 1992, one geologist wrote: "The biggest spines found were about 9 inches long, **shaped a little like a shark's dorsal fin**. The smallest, at tail-tip, were about 3 inches high." We must ask: how could these ancient Indians have known how to draw these creatures if they never had seen them firsthand (or had them described to them by someone who had seen them)?

"The biggest spines found were about 9 inches long, shaped a little like a shark's dorsal fin."

HERODOTUS AND FLYING SNAKES

Herodotus

One ancient historian named Herodotus wrote about events that happened in approximately 450 B.C. In his book, he mentioned flying snakes.

> There is a place in Arabia...to which I went, on hearing of some winged serpents; and when I arrived there, I saw bones and spines of serpents, in such quantities as it would be impossible to describe. The form of the serpent is like that of a water-snake; but he has wings without feathers, and as like as possible to the wings of a bat.

Herodotus knew of flying reptiles. He knew these creatures were not birds, mammals, or insects—but reptiles with wings.

There is much more evidence which shows that humans lived with dinosaurs and other extinct reptiles. The reason you do not see it in your school science books is because it stands opposed to evolution. The carvings, stones, figurines, and book references show that humans and dinosaurs did live together in the past. They were not separated by millions of years. When we look at the evidence, we can see the truth.

DINOSAUR SOFT TISSUE

What happens to a chicken bone that gets left outside in the yard? Most of the time a dog or cat eats it or buries it in the ground. But what would happen if it were buried very quickly? It might turn into a chicken-bone fossil. A fossil is something that is left by a plant, animal, or person. When a fossil forms, the bone and stuff inside the bone (like bone marrow or blood cells) are replaced by minerals that are hard like rock. The minerals form in the exact shape of the bone. So, if our chicken bone fossilized, we would dig up a very hard, rocky replica of our bone.

This process sometimes occurred with dinosaur bones. They are buried in the ground and the actual bones, blood cells, and bone marrow are replaced with minerals. Have you ever wondered how old these fossils from dinosaurs are? Scientists who believe in evolution tell us that the fossils from dinosaurs are over 60 million years old. But that simply is not true.

Recently, something happened that helps disprove the idea that dinosaur bones are millions of years old. Scientists uncovered a fossil from a *Tyrannosaurus rex*. But when they broke the fossil open, it still had soft tissues. They had not been completely replaced by rocky minerals. We know that soft tissue could not last millions of years buried under ground. It would have decayed or been fossilized.

Evolutionary scientists should admit that they are wrong. They should admit that dinosaur bones are not millions of years old. But that is not what they have done. Instead, they have said that the soft tissue somehow lasted 65 million years. But that cannot be true. An honest person who found soft tissue in a dinosaur fossil would admit that the fossil could not be millions of years old. This find helps us to see that dinosaurs did not live millions of years ago, but were created by God only a few thousand years ago, during the Creation week we read about in Genesis 1.

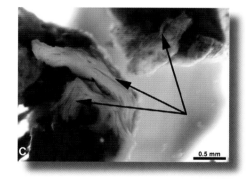

COULD HUMANS REALLY HAVE LIVED WITH DINOSAURS?

Why is it so hard for most people to believe that dinosaurs and humans once lived together? One of the main reasons is because people living in the 21st century are used to thinking that all dinosaurs were enormous kill-

ing machines. People think that they would have killed all of the humans by biting them in half with their super-sized teeth, or by hunting them down and cutting them open with five-inch-long claws. People think that the large plant eaters would have crushed humans with their massive feet or by striking them with their huge tails. Humans are just too small, unintelligent, and scrawny to have lived during the time of the dinosaurs, right? That seems to be the way many evolutionary scientists, movie makers, and magazine editors portray these terrible lizards. But that idea is wrong.

Truly, dinosaurs were amazing creatures. But have you ever stopped to consider what kind of mighty creatures humans live with on the Earth today? Elephants, for example, are the largest land-living animals in the world today. Some reach weights of up to 22,000 pounds, and could easily crush a man just by stepping on him. Yet, for thousands of years humans have been known to live with, and tame, these creatures. Over 2,200 years ago, the empire of Carthage used tamed African elephants (the largest elephants in the world) to battle the Romans. Today, many elephants are still being controlled by man. Tamed elephants are used in

The idea that all dinosaurs were vicious meat-eating killers is simply untrue.

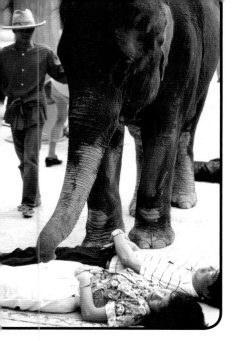

various Asian countries to perform in religious ceremonies, or to do physical labor like hauling lumber or transporting people from place to place. Tamed elephants are also frequently seen performing at circuses.

Humans have been able to live alongside elephants for thousands of years. Some humans and elephants have even become good "friends." So why is it so hard for people to think of humans living next to some of the large dinosaurs? Yes, some dinosaurs like *Brachiosaurus* grew to be about four times larger than the largest elephants. But, if man can work with, play, and go to battle alongside (or on top of) elephants—the largest land animals on Earth today—it surely is not absurd to think humans did similar things with certain dinosaurs.

Whales are the largest animals that have ever existed on Earth—larger than any elephant or dinosaur. Blue whales have been known to weigh as much as 400,000 pounds, have a heart the size of a small car, and possess a tongue large enough to hold 50 people. Yet, humans have hunted many species of whales for centuries. Some people today ride in small boats or swim next to some of these massive creatures.

Killer whales are another one of God's magnificent creatures that live with us on this Earth. Killer whales are one of the oceans' fiercest predators, and are able to kill much larger whales when swimming in packs (known as "pods"). Killer whales hunt so well that very few animals can escape from them. Killer whales eat thousands of pounds of mammal meat every year. Seals, sea lions, walruses, otters, polar bears, and

Questions to Consider

◇ What are some jobs that ancient people might have used dinosaurs to perform?

◇ Why do you think that most people incorrectly assume dinosaurs and humans could not have lived together?

◇ What are some ways humans could have captured, trained, trapped, or avoided dinosaurs? [Clue: Think about how people work with dangerous creatures today.]

even moose have all been found in the stomachs of these vicious creatures.

Amazingly, these large "killing machines" (weighing as much as 10,000 pounds) can be captured, tamed, and trained to do all sorts of things. The famous orcas living at Sea World in Orlando, Florida, occasionally take their trainers for rides on their backs. Trainers of killer whales have even been known to stick their heads inside the whales' mouths (which usually hold about 40-56 large, 3-inch-long teeth) without getting bitten.

How can a 150-pound man teach a 10,000-pound whale how to jump over hurdles, ring bells, and perform

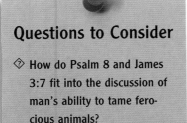

Questions to Consider

◇ How do Psalm 8 and James 3:7 fit into the discussion of man's ability to tame ferocious animals?

other neat tricks without being harmed? The answer is found (at least partly) in Genesis 1:27-28:

> So God created man in His own image; in the image of God He created him; male and female He created them. Then God blessed them, and God said to them, "Be fruitful and multiply; fill the earth and **subdue** it; have **dominion** over the fish of the sea, over the birds of the air, and over every living thing that moves on the earth."

The reason man can tame even the largest and most vicious creatures on Earth is because God created man higher than animals, and gave him the ability to "subdue" them and have "dominion" over them.

If man can live with and tame such amazing creatures as the elephant, the blue whale, the killer whale, lions, tigers, and bears, it should not be hard to understand that man could have lived with, and possibly even tamed, the dinosaurs.

WRONG IDEAS ABOUT DINOSAUR EXTINCTION

It seems that no one wants to know why the saber-toothed tiger became extinct. And rarely do people question why the woolly mammoth died out. But everyone wants to know what happened to the dinosaurs!

Why are dinosaurs no longer on the Earth? What drove them into extinction? The truth is, no one knows for sure why all the dinosaurs died out, although many people who believe in evolution have suggested a number of reasons.

Some believe that small, rat-like mammals evolved, and ate all of the dinosaur eggs until none was left. Others think that a terrible disease struck the dinosaurs, resulting in worldwide extinction. Some scientists say that the oxygen levels in the air were much higher when the dinosaurs lived than they are now. And as the oxygen levels decreased over time to current levels, dinosaurs found it harder and harder to breathe, and eventually became extinct.

The most widely accepted theory is that an asteroid the size of a large city (about 6 miles in diameter) smashed into the Earth, starting fires and throwing tons of dust into the air. The smoke and dust was then carried around the planet by jet stream winds, and it soon stopped much of the Sun's rays from reaching the ground. Without enough sunshine, most of the plants died, and the Earth got very cold. According to this theory, the dinosaurs finally became extinct, because they

> **Some believe that small, rat-like mammals evolved, and ate all of the dinosaur eggs until none was left.**

could not live without food and warmth, which became scarce as a result of the asteroid.

Like the other theories already mentioned, the asteroid theory has a lot of problems. First, no one knows why this huge space object would kill every dinosaur (large and small), but leave many other forms of life unharmed. Why did the asteroid not kill other reptiles, like turtles and alligators? Second, there is nothing in the fossil record that supports the death of all of the dinosaurs at almost the same time. Even though many dinosaurs are found in fossil "graveyards" throughout the world, the evidence also shows that some lived at a later time. And finally, the possible collision site where some scientists think the asteroid struck [called Chicxulub (CHEEK-shoe-lube)] may not have even been created by an asteroid. Scientists cannot deny that the crater could have been caused by some kind of geologic activity.

Why did the asteroid not kill other reptiles, like turtles and alligators?

DINOSAUR GRAVEYARDS AND THE FLOOD

One of the greatest mysteries concerning the dinosaurs is the large number of dinosaur graveyards found in different parts of the world. Dinosaur fossils have been discovered as far north as the Arctic, as far south as Antarctica, and almost everywhere in between. In fact, dinosaur fossils have been found on all seven continents. Nearly 100 years ago, a dinosaur graveyard was found in Tanzania, Africa. Literally tons of fossils and rocks were mined and sent to Berlin, Germany, for display. At Dinosaur National Monument on the Colorado/Utah border, more than 300 dinosaurs of many different kinds have been excavated. Another site in Utah has produced 10,000 dinosaur bones that were extracted from the rock. The burial of such large numbers of dinosaurs in various locations all over the world demands a good answer.

Because most scholars believe the fossilization of bones usually requires large quantities of water, many scientists think that local flash floods caused large herds of dinosaurs to drown. (This is the explanation given at the Dinosaur National Monument fossil quarry as to why 1,600 fossilized dinosaur bones are buried there). Others think that some of the graveyards resulted from animals attempting to cross flooded rivers. No doubt, such localized disasters have occurred throughout the world, just as they still occur today from time to time. But, the problem with these theories is that while they may explain the death of some dinosaurs in some places, they don't adequately explain the existence of dinosaur graveyards throughout the whole world.

The law of cause and effect states that every material effect must have an adequate cause that comes before the effect. Your dad's car was not crushed because a fly landed on it, and your sister did not suffer a broken ankle because she stepped on an ant. These are not adequate causes. (The car may have been crushed

Extra Evidence

➤ On the wall opposite the fossils at the Dinosaur National Monument fossil quarry, a large painting shows a picture of what scientists think caused the fossils to form. Notice that the writing displayed near the picture suggests that the fossils formed during a flood. We have circled the words in the paragraph that explain the scenario. While the comments on the millions of years is incorrect, the idea that a flood caused the fossils fits perfectly with the biblical idea of Noah's Flood.

After a seasonal flood: This scene of 145 million years ago is based on clues found in the rock face behind you.

Carcasses brought downstream by the fast-moving, muddy water were washed onto a sandbar. Some were buried completely by tons of sand — their bones preserved in a near-perfect state. The bones of others, closer to the surface, were jumbled and damaged by scavengers and moving water.

The illustration below is one artist's idea of what may have happened to most dinosaurs during the Flood of Noah.

because a semi-truck ran into it, but not because a bug hit it!) Likewise, the huge dinosaur graveyards are an effect of some type of adequate cause. What was that "cause"?

The fossilized bones of dinosaurs found in graveyards throughout the world are probably best explained by the worldwide Flood of Noah's day (see Genesis 6-8), not by localized floods scattered throughout history. In Genesis 7:19, the Bible explains that during the Flood of Noah's day "all the high hills under the whole heaven were covered." As we think about this verse, we realize that the most difficult thing for any flood to cover is a high hill. In fact, most floods do not cover high hills; they cover lower areas of land like valleys or plains. If the high hills were covered, then all of the area that was lower than the hills had to be covered as well. As we look closer at this verse, we see that

all of the high hills under the **whole** heaven were covered. Not one single hill on the entire Earth was left dry. That would mean that the only dry area on the globe would have been inside Noah's ark.

During that year-long global Flood, thousands of dinosaurs drowned, and their bones were buried very quickly in muddy deposits. This would account for the chaotic jumble of dinosaur bones found in bone beds in various parts of the world—from Alberta, Canada, to Tanzania, Africa. Although the Flood did not destroy all of the dinosaurs (some would have been on Noah's ark), it is the best explanation as to why so many of these giant reptiles throughout the world were rapidly overwhelmed, buried, and fossilized.

WHERE DID THE DINOSAURS GO?

So why did dinosaurs eventually become extinct if some did survive the Flood? One reason may be that the dinosaurs which survived the Flood on Noah's ark were not able to cope very well in the new world, because the climate was so different. One indication that the world was very different after the Flood comes from an understanding of how the ages of people at their deaths decreased by hundreds of years. Before the Flood, the Bible indicates that men lived to be 800 and 900 years old (see Genesis 5:3-32). In fact, the grandfather of Noah, whose name was Methuselah, lived to be 969 years old (that's almost a millennium!). After the Flood, however, people began dying at much younger ages. Instead of living to be 800 or 900 years old, the descendants of Noah eventually began living to be only 150 to 200 years old.

Extra Evidence

➤ Fossilized remains of various marine animals have been found on the tops of some of the world's highest mountains. The Global Flood provides an excellent explanation for such fossils.

For example, Abraham died at age 185 (Genesis 25:7). Although that may sound old to us today, compared to the ages of people before the Flood, it is much younger. Many creation scientists believe that the same conditions that caused man's lifespan to decrease were the same conditions that eventually (years later) drove the dinosaurs to extinction.

The last surviving dinosaurs may have become extinct for the same reason that many other animals through the years have died out—the filling of our planet with humans. It is very possible that humans hunted various

Extra Evidence

➢ To some people, the idea of dinosaurs on Noah's Ark seems absurd. However, it is not so hard to accept when all the evidence is examined. First, we must remember that God is the Creator of all the animals, and He knew exactly how big the Ark needed to be. With a total volume of about 1.5 million cubic feet of space, the Ark was large enough to accomplish its purpose. Second, not all dinosaurs were massive in size. Some were only the size of dogs or even chickens. Finally, it is possible that God told Noah to take younger, smaller dinosaurs, instead of older, larger ones.

kinds of dinosaurs into extinction. Certain species of tigers, bears, elephants, and hippos have all been hunted almost to the brink of destruction. Perhaps the same thing happened to many kinds of dinosaurs. Immediately after the Flood, God said to Noah and his family:

> The fear of you and the dread of you shall be on every beast of the earth, on every bird of the air, on all that move on the earth, and on all the fish of the sea. They are given into your hand. Every moving thing that lives shall be food for you. I have given you all things, even as the green herbs (Genesis 9:2-3).

It was not until after the Flood that we read of God granting humans permission to hunt animals. Soon, mighty men like Nimrod, a grandson of Ham, began hunting the various animals of the Earth (Genesis 10:8-12). Although dinosaurs did repopulate in various places throughout the world after the Flood, it could be that many eventually died out at the hands of hunters. Countries all over the world have stories of dragon slayers. Perhaps there is at least some truth to them.

CHAPTER REVIEW

FILL IN THE BLANKS

1. Most science books tell us that dinosaurs lived _____ of years before humans ever arrived on Earth.

2. Several *Diplodocus*-like dinosaurs on the Ica stones have what appear to be dermal _____—something never previously reported by scientists until 1992.

3. Evolutionist Francis Barnes made the following statement regarding the rock art at Kachina Bridge: "There is a petroglyph in Natural Bridges National Monument that bears a startling resemblance to a _____, specifically a *Brontosaurus*, with long tail and neck, small head and all."

4. One indication that the world was very different after the Flood comes from an understanding of how the ages of people at their deaths decreased by _____ of years.

5. It is very possible that humans _____ various kinds of dinosaurs into extinction.

6. Many dinosaur clay figurines have been unearthed in _____, Mexico since 1944.

SHORT ANSWER

1. Why is the dinosaur petroglyph at Natural Bridges National Monument good evidence for the coexistence of dinosaurs and humans?

2. Why is it so hard for many people to believe that dinosaurs and humans once lived together?

3. What are some amazing animals with which we live on this planet today?

4. Why is it logical to believe that man could have lived with dinosaurs in the past?

5. Why does the asteroid theory not adequately explain the extinction of the dinosaurs?

6. List some possible reasons why dinosaurs eventually became extinct if some survived the Flood.

7. Why is it logical to believe that man could have tamed certain dinosaurs?

8. Why are the Ica Burial stones good evidence for the coexistence of dinosaurs and humans?

TRUE/FALSE

1. ____ Humans never lived with dinosaurs.

2. ____ The dinosaur petroglyph at Natural Bridges National Monument shows every sign of being an actual drawing of a real dinosaur by people who lived in that area long before the first dinosaur fossil was found in modern times.

3. ____ Fossilized *Apatosaurus* bones were found only about 45 miles from the dinosaur petroglyph at Natural Bridges National Monument.

4. ____ Samuel Hubbard and his coworkers found several fossilized dinosaur footprints within several miles of the dinosaur drawing at the Havai Supai Canyon.

5. ____ Some elephants reach weights up to 22,000 pounds.

6. ____ It is absurd to believe that humans ever tamed any dinosaurs.

7. ____ It is a proven fact that dinosaurs became extinct because an asteroid the size of a large city smashed into the Earth.

8. ____ Dinosaur fossils have been found only in North America.

9. ____ The fossilized bones of dinosaurs found in graveyards throughout the world are probably best explained by the worldwide Flood of Noah's day, not by localized floods scattered throughout history.

MULTIPLE CHOICE

1. Rock carvings are called
   A. Pictographs
   B. Petroglyphs
   C. Sketches
   D. Murals

2. In 1924, this man discovered a carving of a creature that looks like a dinosaur in the Havai Supai Canyon
   A. Herodotus
   B. Javier Cabrera Darquea
   C. Waldemar Julsrud
   D. Samuel Hubbard

3. Evolutionary rock-art expert, Dennis Slifer, stated that there is a curious petroglyph in Natural Bridges National Monument that looks like a
   A. Giraffe
   B. Horse
   C. Dinosaur
   D. None of the above

4. Herodotus wrote about seeing
   A. Reptiles with wings
   B. Bats
   C. Lizards
   D. None of the above

5. The more popular name for *Apatosaurus*
   A. *Brontosaurus*
   B. *Allosaurus*
   C. *Triceratops*
   D. *Velociraptor*

6. The largest animals ever known to exist on Earth
   A. Dinosaurs
   B. Elephants
   C. Blue whales
   D. None of the above

7. Many scientists believe that dinosaur graveyards were caused by
   A. Localized flash floods
   B. Tornadoes
   C. Hurricanes
   D. Volcanoes

8. One geologist reported that the dermal spines on the backs of certain long-neck dinosaurs were shaped a little like a
   A. Tulip
   B. Shark's dorsal fin
   C. Beaver's tail
   D. Cactus

134   Chapter—7 *Dinosaurs and Man*

CHAPTER–8
EVOLUTION IS NOT A PROVEN FACT

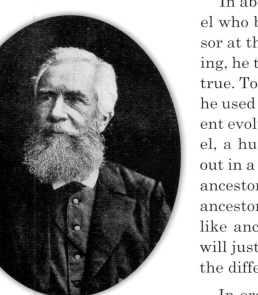

While evolutionists confidently claim that the **theory** of evolution is actually a **fact** of science, the available evidence says otherwise. Not only is the "fact" of evolution based upon non-provable assumptions that are not capable of being tested and proven using the scientific method, and not only do natural laws contradict evolutionary thought (like the Law of Biogenesis and the Law of Cause and Effect), but the evidences given to support the theory of evolution in textbooks, journals, and lectures throughout the world are full of mistakes and untruths. Many of the "proofs" used to spread the theory of evolution have been known by evolutionists for decades to be false, and still those proofs continue to be used. Notice the real facts behind some of evolution's most often used "proofs."

ERNST HAECKEL'S HOAX

In about 1860, there was a man named Ernst Haeckel who believed in evolution. He was a German professor at the University of Jena. During his years of teaching, he tried to convince his students that evolution was true. To "prove" this to his students and fellow teachers, he used the idea that a human baby goes through different evolutionary stages as it grows. According to Haeckel, a human embryo (a baby in its early stages) starts out in a one-celled stage, just as its ancient amoeba-like ancestor. It develops gill slits, just like its ancient fish ancestor. And it even has a tail, just as its ancient ape-like ancestor. Therefore, suggested Dr. Haeckel, if we will just watch a human embryo grow, then we will see the different stages of evolution.

In order to prove his theory, he made several drawings of the different stages. But when he published these drawings, other professors began to question

Ernst Haeckel

Haeckel's accuracy. Upon further investigation, it was discovered that Dr. Haeckel had not only been **inaccurate**, but he had even been **dishonest**. Other science professors charged Haeckel with fraud. When confronted with the charge, he confessed that he faked some of his drawings. He also took the drawings from other people and changed them to "prove" his theory. And if that were not bad enough, in one case he used the same picture three different times, and labeled one a human, the second a dog, and the third a rabbit. With all this evidence against him, Haeckel was easily shown to be a fraud.

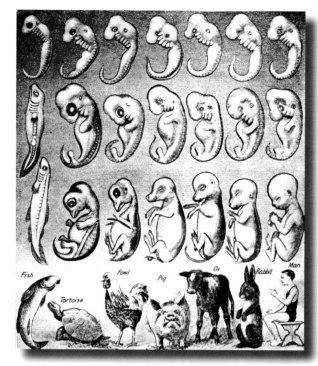

That should be the end of the story, but it is not. Even though Haeckel's false theory and drawings were disproved over 150 years ago, they are still being used today in many science textbooks to "prove" evolution. Other books do not use Haeckel's exact drawings, but they do suggest that humans go through different evolutionary stages as they grow from an embryo. However, today we know for certain that humans do not go through any other "animal" stages as they grow. A human embryo starts as a human, ends as a human, and is a human the entire time. Human embryos never have gill slits like fish as some textbooks suggest, and they do not ever go through a "rabbit-like" stage or a "lizard-like" stage. Humans are humans.

Why are textbook writers still using drawings that were faked, altered, and falsified? That is the real mystery. The next time you see these fake drawings, remember that Ernst Haeckel lied to us about evolution.

The English peppered moth has been used in many science books to "prove" that evolution occurs. According to evolutionists, before the industrial revolution in England, most of these moths were a light, speckled-gray color. Their light color supposedly blended in with the tree trunks, which camouflaged them from birds. A dark form of the moth also existed, but supposedly it was rare because birds could see it easier and eat it. However, when the industrial factories in England started producing soot and smoke, the trees began to turn black. Due to this change, the light-colored moths became easier to see, and the darker moths became camouflaged. In only a few years, the black moths greatly outnumbered the white moths. This change in the moth population proves that species can "evolve" different characteristics that allow them to survive—at least that is the story told by evolutionists in many science books.

But this "proof" of evolution doesn't really prove anything. First of all, during the forty years of research on the moths, very few have ever been found resting on tree trunks during the day. So how did the science-book authors get pictures of the moths on trees? **They either pinned or glued dead**

moths on the tree trunks, or they captured moths and forced them to stay on the trunks. The theory about the camouflage was totally false. And, even though many of the writers and science-book publishers **knew it was false, they used it anyway**.

Second, dark moths and light moths had always been around. No new genetic material was created to form a black moth. Also, **the moths were still moths!** They did not change into lizards or mice. The moth population always had the built-in ability to vary in color, but the moths never had the ability to become anything other than moths.

Those who believe in evolution are terribly mistaken in their thinking. They think that if nature can change an animal a little bit over time, then it can change that animal into a new animal over a long period of time. Evolutionists do not seem to realize that small changes have **limits**. For instance, suppose it takes you nine minutes to run one mile. But you decide to exercise and get into shape, and every week for the first three weeks you run the mile one minute faster. Does that mean that you will be running the mile in **zero** minutes by the ninth week of your training? Of course it doesn't. Eventually you will reach a point when you cannot run any faster.

Moths may change color or size over several generations, but they will never become anything other than a...moth!

Eventually

you will reach a point when you cannot run any faster.

DID HORSES EVOLVE?

One of the most commonly used "proofs" of evolution is a series of horse-like animals. Using a hodge-podge of fossils, evolutionists claim that the modern horse can be traced back to a tiny, four-toed, fox-like animal named *Hyracotherium* (sometimes called *Eohippus*) that is said to have lived about 60 million years ago. Supposedly, the animal started out only 24 inches tall and evolved into the modern-day horse (known as *Equus*) while losing all of its toes in the process.

The problem with this theory is that there simply is no proof for it. The fossil record does not show a sequence of transitional fossils for horses (or **any** species for that matter). The horse series was constructed from fossils (found in many different parts of the world) **that do not fit together**. The creatures that certain science textbooks identify as belonging to the horse family show no ancestor-descendant relationship with one another. For instance, the animals have different num-

|||||||||||||||||||||||||||||||||||||||||||||||||||

The horse series was constructed from fossils that do not fit together!

|||||||||||||||||||||||||||||||||||||||||||||||||||

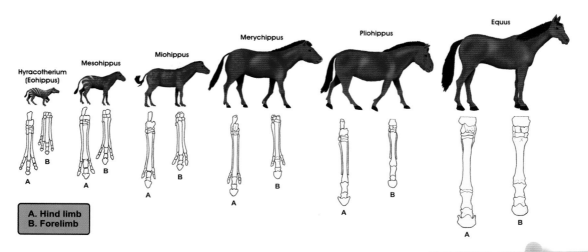

Hyracotherium (Eohippus)
Mesohippus
Miohippus
Merychippus
Pliohippus
Equus

A. Hind limb
B. Forelimb

bers of ribs and vertebrae, but they were supposed to have evolved from one another? Nonsense! The fox-like animal named *Hyracotherium*, which supposedly is the "great-great-granddaddy" of all horses, really has no more resemblance to the horse than it does to any four-legged animal that feeds on vegetation.

Even George Gaylord Simpson, one of the most famous evolutionists of the twentieth century, admitted that the case for horse evolution is nonexistent. He stated: "The uniform, continuous transformation of *Hyracotherium* into *Equus*, so dear to the hearts of generations of textbook writers, **never happened in nature**." Horses have always been horses.

Extra Evidence

➢ A few science textbooks have ceased using the false information about horse evolution because scientists have learned that it is incorrect.

➢ As a replacement for horse evolution, some textbooks are now including material on alleged camel evolution, which has problems similar to those of the horse series.

DID WHALES EVOLVE?

The idea that whales evolved has made headlines numerous times in recent years. Fossil discoveries in Pakistan, and problems with the famous line of horse evolution, have caused scientists to look for other "proofs" of evolution. Supposedly, this new proof can be seen in a gradual change of land animals into whales. Evolutionists believe that a small animal that looked like a wolf or fox began eating fish instead of other animals.

After spending more and more time in shallow water catching fish, this fox-like creature somehow became amphibious—spending part of its life in water, and part on land. Millions of years later, the animal's front legs developed into flippers, the back legs disappeared completely, and the tail developed into a giant fluke.

To "prove" this scenario, evolutionists have pointed to several fossil skeletons, such as the one known as *Pakicetus*. Evolutionists are fond of producing full-color pictures of these "transition" animals, along with fully reconstructed skeletons based on the fossils. What they do not tell you, however, is that most of those pictures are based on only a few bones, not complete skeletons, and that the arguments made revolve around the shape of a few teeth. Their "proof" is mainly bound up in the work of an artist with a good imagination.

The truth is that God made whales with many specialized features that could not have evolved by chance. It would be impossible for a land animal to gradually adjust to the many changes necessary to become a water-living animal. The body must be able to withstand freezing cold water and incredible water pressure—pressure that would quickly kill a human and most animals. A whale's nose hole is on the top of its head so that it can surface and breathe quickly. The backbones of whales are stiff and fused in some places to support the huge muscles needed to propel the giants through the waters. Perhaps the most difficult thing of all for evolution to explain is that all baby mammals born on land suck milk from their mother's breast, but the mother whale (called a cow) has to pump the milk into its baby's mouth so that it does not suck in water and die.

Evolution fails to explain the origin and special features of whales. It is clear from the evidence that the Creator specially designed whales to live in their watery home. They are perfectly fitted for it, and they remind us that God has a place for everyone and everything.

The proof for whale evolution is mainly bound up in the work of an artist with a good imagination.

ARE THINGS THAT LOOK SIMILAR ALWAYS RELATED?

Sometimes you might see a person with an identical twin brother or sister. It is easy to tell that they are related because they look so much alike. Mothers and daughters often look alike, and so do fathers and sons (or even some cousins). Many times, even animals that look similar are often related to each other. Two black rabbits often have baby black rabbits, and two short dogs often produce puppies that are short like them.

The idea that similarity often shows relationship is one of the arguments evolutionists use to "prove" evolu-

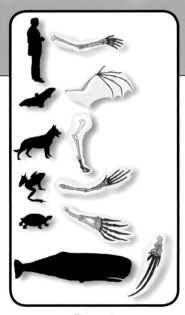

Figure 1

tion. As scientists have worked in various fields, they have learned that there are basic similarities between certain groups. Scientists call these similarities "homologous" structures. Homologous simply means similar. For instance, the wing of the bat, the forefoot of the turtle and the frog, and the arm of the man all have the same general structure (Figure 1 on previous page). Evolutionists also note that the forefoot of the dog, the flipper of the whale, and the hand of man contain basically the same bones and muscles. Therefore, evolutionists conclude that all these animals must be related.

How do creationists respond to such an argument? Well, they certainly do not deny the fact that similarities do exist. It is here, however that a valuable lesson can be learned in the creation/evolution controversy: rarely are the **facts** in dispute—rather, it is the **interpretation** placed on the facts that is in dispute. When the creationist looks at the similarities that exist, instead of claiming common ancestry he says that the evidence points to a common designer. For example, many GMC automobiles have the same wheels, body shapes, and brake systems. Why? Because they were designed by the same company. And they were designed to be able to drive on the same roads and freeways. When the Creator designed a lung, brain, or nervous system that worked well, wouldn't it make sense that He would use these features in different animals that would all live in the same environment, breathe the same air, and eat the same food? Similarity does not always show common **ancestry**; many times it shows common **design**.

In fact, when you honestly look at all similarities, they obviously do not show common ancestry. For example the octopus eye, pig heart, Pekingese dog's face, and donkey's milk all have similar parallel structures in the human body, but even evolutionists would deny the living animals in which they are found are closely related to each other or to humans.

Many things in nature have similar structures. But those structures did not evolve and they do not prove that the different animals and humans are distant relatives. In fact, the common structures found among the animals and humans point to the fact that all animals, plants, and humans have a common Designer.

...the octopus eye, pig heart, Pekingese dog's face, and donkey's milk all have similar parallel structures in the human body.

ARE THERE "LEFTOVERS" OF EVOLUTION?

Have you ever seen a birthday balloon hanging on someone's mailbox—a balloon that once had helium in it, but had been there so long that the helium had leaked out? The poor balloon sagged to the ground, all wrinkled and good for nothing. It once was a very useful, floating balloon. Now it is a useless, wrinkly mess of rubber.

Now think with us about the theory of evolution. According to evolution, animals and humans have been evolving for millions of years. Supposedly, they started out very simple, but over millions of years have progressed into the complex creatures we see today. If this really did happen, the theory of evolution says that we should find some "leftover" structures that once were used but are not used anymore, just like the saggy, useless balloon. The "leftover" structures might be body organs or parts that were used "millions of years ago" by an animal or human, but now the creature has changed so much that the structure is no longer needed. Evolutionists call these leftovers "vestigial" (ve-STIJ-al) organs.

A vestige is a piece or part left by something. For instance, after a war, old land mines accidentally left in a field would be a vestige of the war. Since evolutionists believe that evolution actually happened, they believe that there are leftover pieces or parts of it—vestiges. That is why evolutionists call certain body parts vestigial; they think the parts are left over from evolution.

There is one problem with this idea of vestigial parts: it is absolutely false! At one time, there was a list of over 100 parts of the human body that scientists believed were useless and vestigial. Included in this list were tonsils, the appendix, wisdom teeth, the coccyx, and hair. After years of research, we have learned that these parts are not leftovers of evolution. In fact, scientists have discovered that many of these parts are **very** important.

The appendix is a small pouch that extends off the large intestine. In recent years, doctors have observed that the appendix is a tough soldier against infection, especially in people who have been exposed to some types of radiation. Inside the appendix is lymphoid (LIM-foid) tissue which helps produce white blood cells that fight disease. Also, early in a child's life the appendix is relatively larger than it is in adults. It is during these early stages of life that the appendix appears to play an even bigger role in guarding the body from infection.

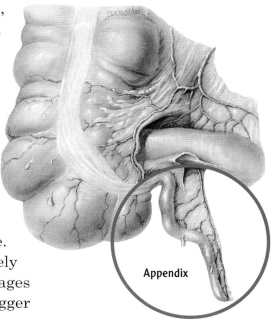

Appendix

Your tonsils are two round, light colored areas that can be found in the back of your throat, one on each side. Like the appendix, most people thought that the tonsils were evidence of evolution, because they supposedly didn't do anything. Scientists now know that tonsils actually do the same thing as the appendix—they help in fighting off germs!

Wisdom teeth (the third row of molars) are one of the most controversial of all the so-called vestigial structures. Evolutionists believe that wisdom teeth devel-

||||||||||||||||||||||||||||||||||||||||||

...scientists have discovered that many alleged "vestigial organs" are very important.

||||||||||||||||||||||||||||||||||||||||||

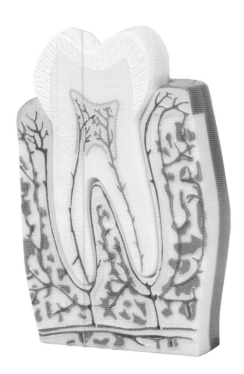

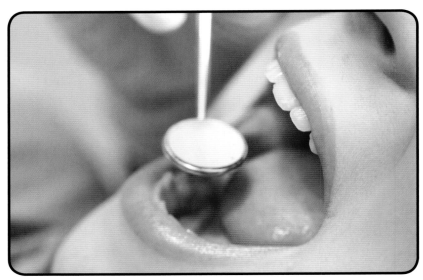

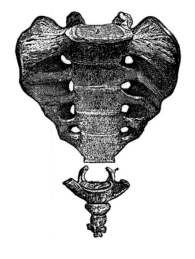

oped thousands of years ago, when human diets con-sisted mostly of raw and unprocessed food that required the extra chewing and grinding power of a third set of molars. Today, some evolutionists call wisdom teeth vestigial structures because they say that the human jaw is getting smaller, and wisdom teeth are no lon-ger needed. Research in recent years has shown that wisdom teeth have the same chewing function as oth-er teeth. Scientists also have found that wisdom teeth often will not damage the position of other teeth in the mouth.

Another so-called vestigial structure in the human body is the coccyx. The coccyx is the small group of bones at the end of the human spine. According to evolution-ists, the coccyx is the left-over part of a tail that serves no purpose now. These evolutionists also say that if the living body had really been created, it would have no useless organs in it, like the coccyx. We now know, however, that the coccyx has a purpose that is very im-portant in human development. The coccyx serves as a point of attachment for several pelvic muscles that help us stand up. Like the shocks on a car, the coccyx also is used as a shock absorber when we sit down. Without it, we would not be able to sit very well or comfortably.

Human body hair also has some important functions, which previously were unknown. First, body hair plays a very important role in the protection of the skin. Body hair functions to warm the skin, and to protect the skin from germs. Hair also can act as a kind of radar, letting us know when something is crawling on us. For instance, sometimes a tick will get on a person and go undetected for a while. Yet, if that tick moves a leg or arm hair too much, we can feel the movement and get rid of the tick. Such are the benefits of having hair.

At one time, all of these parts looked useless to us, because we had not studied them closely enough. After years of observation and testing, scientists are now beginning to realize that the parts they once considered useless are quite helpful. Just because we do not know a body part's function does not mean it is useless. God designed the body perfectly. There are no leftovers of evolution. As the psalmist wrote, humans are "fearfully and wonderfully made" (Psalm 139:14). Creationists recognize that the word "vestigial" does not really stand for "useless organ," but instead, is used to describe an organ that's intended purpose is not (yet) known.

Powerful Point

☑ If man does have over 100 vestigial organs, then in the past he would have had more organs than he now has. In the past, he would have been developing the organs that he presently has, plus he would have had the 100+ functional vestigial organs. So the farther back we go in time, the more complex the organism becomes. Yet, evolutionary theory states that organisms become more complex over time. How can both of these teachings be correct? Evolution is the rise of new, different, and functioning organs, not the wasting away of already-present, complex organs.

||||||||||||||||||||||||||||||||||||||||||||

God designed the body perfectly. There are no leftovers of evolution.

||||||||||||||||||||||||||||||||||||||||||||||

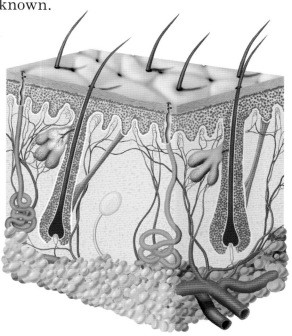

Extra Evidence: Whale Legs and Snake Legs

Whales are amazing creatures. The smallest whales are only eight and a half feet long, while the biggest whale, the 110-foot-long blue whale, is bigger than any of the dinosaurs were! Whales are unique, in that they are marine mammals (most mammals live on land). Whales cause big problems for evolutionists, because evolution says that mammals evolved on land and some moved into the ocean after they evolved the special features required for underwater life. Evolutionists support their idea by pointing out that some whales have tiny "legs" that were supposedly once used for walking, but are of no use anymore. Scientists claim that the legs of whales are "leftovers" of evolution.

Hillary Mayell wrote in *National Geographic* that today's sperm whales have vestigial hind legs. But the legs that Mrs. Mayell claimed are useless actually do have a purpose. The tiny hind legs of the whale help it to reproduce. Evolutionists themselves are forced to admit this fact. The fact is, God created things to serve a purpose, and the whales' legs are no exception.

Evolutionists often try to find what they want to find, and many times end up ignoring the actual facts. This is what some scientists do concerning snake legs. Snakes have what appear to be the "stump" of legs toward the back of their bodies. Evolutionary scientists claim that snakes were once lizards, but due to the processes of evolution, they lost their legs, and now they are left with nothing but short, useless limbs that simply "stick out." This is untrue.

Scientists have discovered that, like the whale, snakes' legs aid in their reproduction. But also, snakes use these short legs in fighting. Amazing! These "vestigial" organs are not vestigial at all. They all serve a purpose. Evolution couldn't make everything "just right." But God, the Great Designer, leaves nothing off, and has nothing left over.

CHAPTER REVIEW

FILL IN THE BLANKS

1. At one time, scientists believed that there were over _____ vestigial organs in the human body.

2. _____ believe that we can trace our ancestry back to a single cell billions of years ago.

3. Similarities between things in nature point to a common _____, not a common ancestor.

4. During the forty years of research on the English Peppered Moth, very ____ moths were ever found resting on tree trunks during the day.

5. Ernst Haeckel was guilty of _____.

6. Researchers have discovered that the _____ helps fight certain types of cancer cells.

7. _____ _____ are some of the most controversial of all the so-called vestigial structures.

8. Humans are "fearfully and _____ made" (Psalm 139:14).

TRUE/FALSE

1. ____ Evolutionists claim that the modern horse can be traced back to a tiny, four-toed, fox-like animal.

2. ____ According to Ernst Haeckel, man is created in the image of God.

3. ____ Moths gradually change color or size over several generations, until they finally become a bird.

4. ____ It does not make sense that God would create animals with similarities.

5. ____ The evolutionary horse series was constructed from fossils found in many different parts of the world that do not fit together.

6. ____ Evolution fails to explain the origin and special features of whales.

7. ____ Creationists believe that humans have body parts that are left over from evolution.

8. ____ The coccyx acts like a shock absorber when we sit down.

SHORT ANSWER

1. What are vestigial organs?

2. Explain why the English Peppered Moth story does not prove evolution.

3. Discuss how the evolutionary idea that organisms become more complex over time conflicts with evolutionists' teachings about vestigial organs.

4. Discuss some of the specialized features of whales.

5. Explain why common structures in animals logically points to a common Creator.

1. A German professor who taught that a human baby goes through different evolutionary stages as it grows
   A. Charles Darwin
   B. Richard Dawkins
   C. Ernst Haeckel
   D. Isaac Newton

2. This female animal pumps milk into its baby's mouth so that it does not suck in water and die
   A. Whale
   B. Dog
   C. Horse
   D. Octopus

3. The small, fox-like animal that allegedly lived 60 million years ago, and was the ancestor of the modern horse
   A. *Hyracotherium*
   B. Dingo
   C. Hyena
   D. *Archaeopteryx*

4. The theory about this little creature being camouflaged by tree trunks was totally false
   A. English Peppered Moth
   B. Squirrel
   C. Woodpecker
   D. Owl

5. Plays a very important role in the protection of skin
   A. Freckles
   B. Hair
   C. Moles
   D. None of the above

6. A piece or part left by something
   A. *Pakicetus*
   B. Embryo
   C. *Eohippus*
   D. Vestige

7. Another name for vestigial
   A. Coccyx
   B. Embryo
   C. Leftover
   D. Haeckel

8. Over time, English Peppered Moths changed into
   A. Birds
   B. Butterflies
   C. Monkeys
   D. None of the above

9. A small pouch that extends off the large intestine
   A. Bladder
   B. Cochlea
   C. Appendix
   D. Tonsil

10. Homologous means
    A. Similar
    B. Different
    C. Change over time
    D. None of the above

11. A baby in its early stages
    A. Embryo
    B. Vestigial
    C. *Eohippus*
    D. None of the above

12. Research in recent years has shown that wisdom teeth
    A. Are leftovers of evolution
    B. Serve no purpose
    C. Should always be removed
    D. Have the same chewing function as other teeth

CHAPTER–9
DID HUMANS EVOLVE?

OUR ALLEGED ANCESTORS

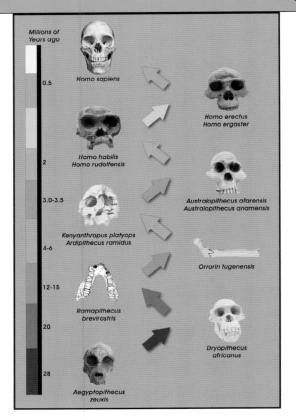

Millions of Years ago

0.5 — Homo sapiens

2 — Homo habilis / Homo rudolfensis

3.0-3.5 — Kenyanthropus platyops / Ardipithecus ramidus

4-6

12-15 — Ramapithecus brevirostris

20

28 — Aegyptopithecus zeuxis

Homo erectus / Homo ergaster

Australopithecus afarensis / Australopithecus anamensis

Orrorin tugenensis

Dryopithecus africanus

We've all seen pictures of our alleged animal ancestors. Normally, artists draw these creatures as hairy animals that share both human and ape-like characteristics, often carrying clubs and living in caves. Most of us can even recognize their names: Neanderthal Man, Nebraska Man, Lucy, *Homo habilis*. But what is the truth about the origin of humans? Did we evolve from ape-like ancestors as many would have us believe, or were we made in the image and likeness of God as Genesis 1:26-27 plainly states? You be the judge. Examine the following evidence, and then make your decision. We think you will see that man did not evolve from ape-like creatures, but instead was created by God.

In looking at the evidence regarding the origin of humans, we first need to dig deeply into the ground. Buried under layers of dirt and rocks we find fossilized skeletons—many of which, once they are discovered, are stored in vaults where they are better protected than gold. However, these skeletons do not look anything like the skeletons you see in sci-

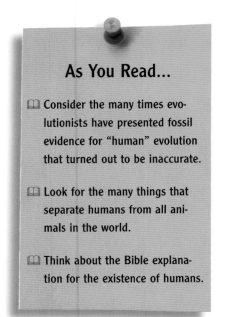

As You Read...

📖 Consider the many times evolutionists have presented fossil evidence for "human" evolution that turned out to be inaccurate.

📖 Look for the many things that separate humans from all animals in the world.

📖 Think about the Bible explanation for the existence of humans.

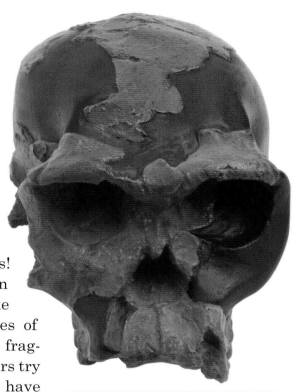

ence classrooms or taped to the wall at Halloween. These skeletons often are crushed by the weight of the dirt and rocks on top of them, and rarely are they complete! Rather than simply digging up a complete skeleton, researchers may find small pieces and fragments of bones scattered over large areas (some as large as a football field!). Often these fossilized bone fragments are put together like a jigsaw puzzle with missing pieces. Occasionally, however, pieces get put together that really belong to two or three different puzzles! But what about all those pictures you've seen on the covers of magazines—those complete ape-like skulls? Often those images were simply pictures of casts that had been created using whatever bone fragments were available. From those casts, researchers try to **imagine** what they believe the creature might have looked like (you know the ones—those hairy creatures that frequently are shown living in caves). These ape-like creatures that were supposed to be the "missing links" between humans and apes are far from it! Look at the evidence.

Notice the grey-blue patches on the skull above. Those are areas where the paleontologist had to guess. Fortunately, this was a nearly complete fossil, or more guess work would have been required.

NEANDERTHAL MAN

This is probably one of the most famous "missing links." We are all familiar with pictures of this hairy, ape-like creature that some might think belongs in a cave. However, after examining the fossil remains, Dr. A.J.E. Cave proved that this **was nothing more than an old man who suffered from arthritis**! Also, remains from "modern humans" have been found near the remains of Neanderthals, which have been dated by evolutionists as being older than those of Neanderthals. What sense does that make? Truly, the "Neanderthal" species is nothing more than modern man.

NEBRASKA MAN

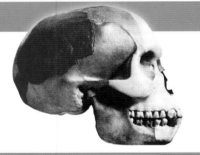

Researchers constructed this "missing link" from a **single tooth**. Pictures were drawn that depicted this ape-like creature (and his family!) gathered around a fire. However, that single tooth later was discovered to be the tooth of an extinct pig! Nebraska Man was not a missing link, but just the figment of an evolutionist's overactive imagination.

This illustration, as well as those of Rhodesian Man, "Lucy," and *Homo habilis*, are what our evolutionary forefathers supposedly looked like. In truth, the pictures are not accurate.

Inner   Anterier   Outer   Posterier

PILTDOWN MAN

Thought to be a genuine missing link for over forty years, it later was determined that someone had forged this particular "discovery" by combining the skull of a human and the jawbone of an ape!

RHODESIAN MAN

This famous skeleton was found in a zinc mine in 1921, and was displayed prominently for years in the British Museum of Natural History. Unfortunately, museum employees who were unfamiliar with human anatomy reconstructed this "ape-man." Since the hipbones were smashed, the designers fashioned this fossil as being stooped over. It wasn't until many years later, when anatomists examined the skeleton, that it was determined to be nothing more than a modern man.

"LUCY"

This is one of the most famous and most complete fossilized skeletons. For many years, scientists believed that this small creature walked uprightly and was one of our ancient ancestors. However, as evidence became available regarding the true position of bones for this small creature, it was obvious that Lucy was nothing more than an ape.

A scientist named Donald Johanson found "Lucy" in 1974. "Lucy" is the name given to a creature Johanson found in Ethiopia. The creature's skeleton was 40% complete—much more complete than other finds. The creature was given the name "Lucy" because it supposedly was a female, and because a song by the Beatles titled "Lucy in the Sky with Diamonds" was playing in his camp the night after he found the creature. [The scientific name for the creature is *Australopithecus afarensis*.] Was "Lucy" a human-like creature that evolved into humans?

After studying "Lucy," scientists learned some very interesting things. First, they learned that the rib cage of this creature was not shaped like a human's. They also learned that the animal had very stiff wrists, unlike humans. The wrists were like a chimpanzee's wrist. Additional research showed that the arm-bones of the creature were very much like chimpanzee arm bones. Finally, scientists found out that "Lucy" was not even a female. "Lucy" was a male creature very similar to a chimpanzee. In fact, in 1996, even Donald Johanson himself said that "Lucy" had been "dethroned" as the "queen" of human evolution. "Lucy" is not an ancestor to humans.

HOMO HABILIS ("HANDY MAN")

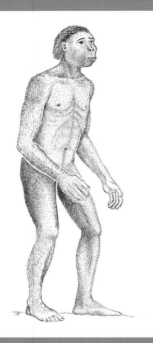

This is the creature that is supposed to have evolved from Lucy. But a fairly complete fossil skeleton of *Homo habilis* was discovered, which indicated that this creature was simply an ape that was in no way related to man. This small fossil is of an adult female that stood only about three feet tall. This is as short as, or shorter than, Lucy. Furthermore, the rest of the skeleton was every bit as primitive, or ape-like, as that of Lucy, who is supposedly two million years older than this adult female *H. habilis*. If evolution were truly taking place, you would expect to see physical changes that make this creature more human-like. No missing link here!

ORCE MAN

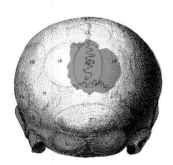

In the early 1980s, a single skull was found near the Spanish town of Orce. Based on this find, some over-eager scientists reconstructed an entire man. For a while, Orce man was said to represent the oldest human fossil ever discovered in Europe. Later, to the embarrassment of many, the bone was identified as being most likely the skull cap of a six-month-old donkey!

FLIPPER MAN?

In 1979, a "collar bone" was found at a site named Sahabi in Libya. Some scientists believed the bone belonged to a primitive ape-man. Using fossilized marine plankton at the site, evolutionists incorrectly dated this new ape-man at 5 million years old. However, this "collar bone" eventually was shown to be the fossilized rib of a marine mammal that was similar to a dolphin!

WHAT'S GOING ON HERE?

Why is there so much confusion regarding human origins? Many people point out that since apes have a lot of the same genetic material as we do (and they do!), they must be our ancestors. And so, each time a skull is dug out of the ground, researchers try to determine just how far along on the evolutionary tree that particular fossil should be placed.

Using evolutionary methods, researchers date the bone fragment they dig up, and then they hire an artist to reconstruct what they believe the creature probably looked like. After that, the animals are written up in scientific journals, where they receive their official names. Often these big scientific names tell us something about where the fossils were found (Neanderthal bones were found in the Neander Valley in Germany) or what the creature may have looked like (*Kenyanthropus platyops* means "flat-faced man from Kenya"). After the material has been dated and named, scientists try to determine where it belongs on their evolutionary tree, which often results in entire limbs being added, moved, or chopped off!

Most all of the alleged human ancestor fossils that have been found up to this point can be placed into one of two groups: apes or humans. A few fossils do have odd characteristics or show abnormal bone structure. But does that mean we evolved? No. It simply means that we have found a variation in bone structure—a variation that you probably can see in your own classroom at school. Some heads are big, some small. Some noses are pointed, and some are flat. Some jawbones look angled, while some look square. Does that

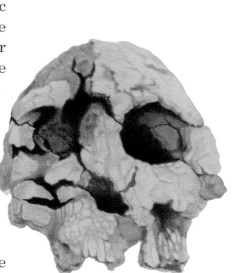

Kenyanthropus platyops

mean some of us still are "evolving," or does it mean that there are occasional differences in humans? Remember this exercise the next time you see a picture of one of those ape-like creatures: look at a skeleton (any one will do) and try to draw the person that used to live with that bony framework. What color was their hair? Was it curly, or straight? Were they male or female? Did they have chubby cheeks, or thin? These are hard questions to answer when we are given only bones to examine. Reconstructions that you see in pictures are not based merely on the fossil **evidence**, but also on ideas of what evolutionists think these creatures may have looked like. The evidence is clear—man did not evolve over millions of years. God, the Giver of life, created the first humans on the sixth day of creation.

> **Reconstructions that you see in pictures are not based merely on the fossil evidence.**

THE LAETOLI FOOTPRINTS

Over two decades ago, the well-known evolutionist Mary Leakey reported finding fossil footprint trails at Laetoli, Tanzania. The strata above the footprints were dated at 3.6 million years, while the strata below them were dated at 3.8 million years. According to Dr. Leakey, these footprints were made, not by *Homo sapiens* (humans), but by some of our early ancestors (like *Australopithecus afarensis*). After all, if these footprints were anywhere close to being 3.6 million years old, then evolutionary theory demands that these prints were not made by humans, since, according to evolution, humans were not around that long ago.

Mary Leakey

One problem with these prints is that they look exactly like human footprints. In fact, one specialist who has done an extensive study of the Laetoli footprints (at the invitation of Mary Leakey) is evolutionist Russell Tuttle. He reported that the individuals who made the tracks were barefoot and probably walked most of the time without shoes. As part of his research, Tuttle observed more than seventy Machiguenga Indians in the rugged mountains of Peru—people who normally walk without shoes. After comparing the footprints of the Indians from Peru with the Laetoli tracks, he wrote: "In discernible features, the Laetoli G prints are indistinguishable from those of habitually barefoot *Homo sapiens.*"

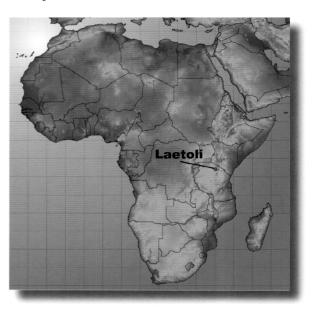

Evolution says that the Laetoli footprints are too old to have been made by humans. If humans really did make these prints, the theory of evolution crumbles. So, most evolutionists reject the obvious **facts** in order to hold on to their **theory**. Although these footprints are still printed in science textbooks as providing evidence for evolution, the truth is, the footprints look exactly like those of modern humans.

FOLLOWING IN YOUR FATHER'S FOOTSTEPS

Most young people at one time or another have tried following in their father's footsteps—literally. If a father is walking through a few inches of snow, many times a child can be seen trying to walk inside the footprints left by his father. But how many times have you seen an animal do this? How many baby chimps have ever purposefully tried walking in their mother's footprints just for the fun of it? From everything we observe in nature, only humans have the tendency to follow their parents in such a way. Interestingly, some of the footprints at Laetoli reveal that one individual actually walked inside the footsteps of another!

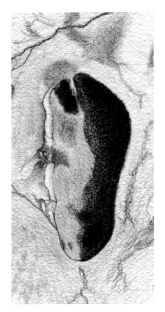

Single Laetoli imprint

ARE APES 99% HUMAN?

For many years, evolutionists claimed that chimpanzees and humans were so similar that they could be considered "kissing cousins." They were quick to point out that the DNA (the genetic material inside a living cell) in humans was almost an identical match to the DNA found in monkeys. In fact, up until 2002, almost any textbook you opened reported that humans and chimpanzees were 98-99% genetically similar. But today, scientists are finding more and more differences in DNA from humans and apes. For instance, a 2002 research study proved that human DNA was at least 5% different from chimpanzees—and that number will probably continue to grow as we learn all of the details about human DNA.

Does it make sense that we share so much DNA with chimpanzees and apes (as well as many other animals?) Well, consider that both humans and chimps are mammals, and possess the same type of internal organs.

Humans and chimps both eat fruits and vegetables, which means that their mouths and digestive systems have to share some similar characteristics. Both humans and chimps get sensory information from their eyes, ears, noses, and fingers. So yes, it would make sense that their DNA has a lot of similarities. But so do many other animals—which explains why humans share a great deal of DNA with all kinds of God's creatures, including the worm! Of the 5,000 best-known human genes, **75%** have matches in the worm. Does this mean that we are 75% identical to a nematode worm? Certainly not. Just because living creatures share some genes with humans does not mean that we are related.

If we took all of the DNA from every cell and then compared the DNA in monkeys and humans, the 4-5% difference in DNA represents approximately **200 million differences in your body compared to an ape!** To help make this number understandable, consider the fact that if evolutionists had to pay you one penny for every one of those differences, you would walk away with $2,000,000. Given those proportions, 4-5% does not appear so small, does it? Man is the only creature that is made in the image and likeness of God. Chimpanzees are simply animals that share some similarities with humans.

CAN MONKEYS DO WHAT HUMANS DO?

Although evolutionists claim that the similarities between humans and chimpanzees prove that we evolved from ape-like creatures, the fact still remains that man can do many things that animals never have been (and never will be) able to do.

Consider, for instance, man's ability to speak. The Bible tells us that Adam was created with this ability "in the beginning." The very day he was created, he named all of the animals before him (Genesis 2:19), and later he used language to offer excuses as to why he disobeyed God. Humans carry on conversations all the time. But when is the last time you heard the monkeys down at the zoo converse with one another using words? Or, when have you ever seen your dog talking to (not barking at) the cat next door? As evolutionist Richard Leakey admitted: "Language does indeed create a gulf between *Homo sapiens* [humans] and the rest of the natural world." The gift of speech is a fundamental part of man's nature that likens him to God and separates him from the rest of creation.

> **How awesome it is to know that we bear God's image!**

Unlike animals, man also is very creative. He has built spaceships that travel 240,000 miles to the Moon; he has made artificial hearts for the sick; and he continues to construct computers that can process billions of pieces of information a second. Animals, on the other hand, cannot do such things because they lack the creative ability that God gave only to man. Beavers may build huts and spiders may weave webs, but they are guided by in-

You've got something in your teeth.

With ears like these, why should I care?

stinct. Thousands of attempts have been made to teach animals to express themselves in art, music, and writing, but none has produced the hoped-for success. Simply put, a huge gap exists between humans and animals in the realm of creativity.

Finally, unlike animals, man has always sought to worship a higher being. Even when he departs from the true God, man still worships something, whether it is a tree, a rock, or even himself. No race or tribe of men anywhere in the world lacks the ability and desire to worship. However, no chimp or dog ever stopped to sing a hymn of praise or offer a prayer of thanks to its Creator.

There is no doubt that man's unique abilities separate him from the animal world and liken him to God. The first chapter of the Bible reveals that humans are created "in the image of God" (Genesis 1:26-27). This does not mean God created us in His physical image, because God is Spirit (John 4:24), and spirits don't have a physical body (Luke 24:39). Instead, we were created with many of the qualities God possesses (though on a different level)—like being able to speak, to create, to love, and to make our own choices. How awesome it is to know that we bear God's image!

IIIIIIIIIIIIIIIIIIIIIIIIIIIIIIIIIIIIIIIIIIIIIIIIIIIIIIIIIIIIIIIIIIIII

"Language does indeed create a gulf between *Homo sapiens* [humans] and the rest of the natural world."

IIIIIIIIIIIIIIIIIIIIIIIIIIIIIIIIIIIIIIIIIIIIIIIIIIIIIIIIIIIIIIIIIIIII

Richard Leakey

THE TRUE STORY OF MAN'S ORIGIN

As we have seen, the idea that humans evolved from ape-like creatures many millions of years ago is false. The true story regarding man's origin can be found only in the Bible.

"In the beginning God created the heavens and the earth." This is the first sentence in Genesis, the first book of the English Bible. The first two chapters of Genesis tell how God created the Sun, Moon, sky, land, plants, animals, and everything in this Universe in six, 24-hour days. But there was one special creature that God created who was not like any of the animals.

On the sixth day of creation, God said "Let Us make man in Our image, according to Our likeness" (Genesis 1:26). In order to make man, God formed him from the dust of the ground and breathed into his nostrils the breath of life. His name was Adam. Adam was God's greatest creation. But there was one problem: Adam was very lonely because none of the other creatures was a suitable helper for him. For this reason, God caused Adam to fall into a deep sleep. As Adam slept, God took one of his ribs and used it to form a woman whom Adam called Eve. Adam and his wife Eve were the first two people to walk on the Earth. They did not evolve from ape-like creatures over a long period of time. God created them on the sixth day of the first week.

CHAPTER REVIEW

FILL IN THE BLANKS

1. Researchers often find small pieces and fragments of _____ scattered over large areas.

2. Remains from "modern humans" have been found near the remains of _____.

3. Researchers constructed _____ man from a **single tooth**.

4. Unlike animals, man always has sought to _____ a higher being.

5. Today, scientists are finding more and more differences in the _____ of humans and apes.

6. Over two decades ago, the well-known evolutionist Mary _____ reported finding fossil footprint trails at Laetoli, Tanzania.

7. In 1996, Donald Johanson admitted that _____ had been "dethroned" as the "queen" of human evolution.

8. Man's unique abilities separate him from the _____ world and liken him to God.

SHORT ANSWER

1. Discuss several differences between the abilities of humans and animals.

2. Knowing that many of the "human ancestors" have been frauds or mistakes, how should that influence a person to approach new findings that are said to be human ancestors?

3. List and discuss several things which show that "Lucy" is not a human ancestor.

4. What does it mean that humans have been made in "the image" of God?

5. Why do many of the pictures of supposed human ancestors fail to tell the true story of the fossils that are actually found?

6. Are the Laetoli footprints evidence for or against the supposed evolution of humans? Give several reasons that confirm your answer.

7. What does the fact that chimpanzees and humans share a large percentage of DNA information prove? What does it fail to prove?

TRUE/FALSE

1. _____ The Laetoli footprints look like those of modern humans.

2. _____ Donald Johanson found Nebraska Man in 1974.

3. _____ Human beings were created in the image of God.

4. _____ Evolutionary science has never made a mistake regarding the origin of humans.

5. _____ Adam and Eve were created by God, and did not evolve from apes.

6. _____ Many pictures drawn from fossil fragments are inaccurate.

7. _____ Neanderthal was a human who suffered from arthritis.

8. _____ It is a proven fact that humans evolved from ape-like creatures.

MULTIPLE CHOICE

1. Humans have a 75% DNA match with which of the following animals?

   A. Shark

   B. Worm

   C. Snake

   D. Octopus

2. This creature was forged from the skull of a human and jawbone of an ape

   A. Nebraska Man

   B. Lucy

   C. Piltdown Man

   D. Orce Man

3. The "collar bone" of one alleged ancestor turned out to be a fossilized rib of a

   A. Man

   B. Gorilla

   C. Chimp

   D. Marine mammal

4. Lucy was discovered by

   A. Donald Johanson

   B. Mary Leakey

   C. Stephen J. Gould

   D. Carl Sagan

5. The Laetoli footprints were discovered by

   A. Donald Johanson

   B. Mary Leakey

   C. Stephen J. Gould

   D. Carl Sagan

6. The Laetoli footprints look like the footprints of modern

   A. Elephants

   B. Humans

   C. Gorillas

   D. Lions

7. This famous skeleton was found in a zinc mine in 1921

   A. Nebraska Man

   B. Lucy

   C. Piltdown Man

   D. Rhodesian Man

8. Supposedly, this creature evolved from Lucy

   A. *Homo Habilis*

   B. Lucy

   C. Piltdown Man

   D. Orce Man

9. According to Jesus (Mark 10:6), humans have been on the Earth

   A. For 4 millions years

   B. Ever since humans evolved from ape-like creatures

   C. From the beginning of the creation

   D. Since shortly after the Big Bang

10. On the sixth day of Creation, God made monkeys, one of which eventually evolved into

    A. Adam

    B. Eve

    C. An early human ancestor known as Lucy

    D. None of the above

11. Evolutionist Richard Leakey admitted that "_____ does indeed create a gulf between *Homo sapiens* [humans] and the rest of the natural world"

    A. Language

    B. Hair

    C. Homology

    D. Bone structure

CHAPTER–10
CREATION SCIENTISTS

LINNÉ
OLJEMÅLNING AF P. KRAFFT D. Ä., 1774
TILLHÖR KUNGL. VET. AKADEMIEN

into the planetary orbits. Kepler's drawing is a pure
is meant to correspond to the actual relation between
orbits. Most important here is the cube, fitted into the

There are thousands of brilliant men and women who believe in creation.

Evolutionist Richard Dawkins once stated: "It is absolutely safe to say that if you meet somebody who claims not to believe in evolution, that person is ignorant, stupid, or insane (or wicked, but I'd rather not consider that)." Dr. Dawkins believes that all smart people believe in evolution. He also believes that anyone who does not believe in evolution is ignorant, insane, or wicked. Is it true that all the smart people believe in evolution? Absolutely not! There are thousands of brilliant men and women who believe in creation. In fact, some of the most brilliant scientists who ever lived believed in God and creation. Let's look at some of those scientists.

WERNHER VON BRAUN (1912-1977)

One of the world's top space scientists was a man by the name of Wernher von Braun. He attended the University of Berlin, and after his graduation began developing rockets for his native country of Germany. However, in 1945 he came to the United States, and ten years later, in 1955, he became a U.S. citizen.

Dr. von Braun was the leading force behind America's own space program. He and his team helped invent and produce the four-stage Jupiter rocket that launched Explorer I, the first United States satellite. In another of his projects, the Saturn V rocket was constructed, eventually putting the first astronauts on the Moon. He directed America's program of missile development for many years, and eventually became the Director of the National Aeronautics and Space Administration (NASA). His office was in Huntsville, Alabama.

During his lifetime, Dr. von Braun received many important honors and awards. But he always gave God credit for his achievements. He believed that the evidence for God's existence could be found all around us in nature. He also believed in the concept of creation as taught in Genesis 1; he did not believe in evolution. He once said that science and religion work so well together that they should be considered as "sisters." The more he studied the heavens, the more evidence he saw of the Creator.

Dr. von Braun was not ashamed of his belief in God. When he died in 1977, coworkers found in his files letters he had written to other scientists (like the famous medical doctor, Albert Schweitzer), in which he tried to show them why they, too, should believe in God. He tried to share his belief in God with people around him. Today, he is remembered as a "giant" in the scientific community, but he also is remembered for his belief in God.

Dr. von Braun was not ashamed of his belief in God.

LOUIS PASTEUR (1822-1895)

One scientist who believed in God became so famous that his name appears on almost every milk container. If you look at the paper carton or plastic jug of milk in your refrigerator, you will see the word "pasteurized." This word comes from the last name of the scientist, Pasteur.

Louis Pasteur was trained in chemistry and physics, but perhaps is best known to us today as the "father of bacteriology." He discovered that many of the diseases that affect humans and animals are the result of dangerous germs that invade the body. He not only discovered many of the bacteria that caused diseases, but was also responsible for developing vaccines to combat them. Have you ever heard of rabies (a disease that causes certain animals to go mad)? Or have you ever heard of diphtheria (an infection that can cause us as humans to get very sick and die)? Louis Pasteur helped

invent vaccines for both of these terrible diseases. Today, most young children in America receive a shot of diphtheria vaccine to protect them against the disease.

During Pasteur's lifetime, many people believed in "spontaneous generation." This is the idea (discussed in chapter two) that nonliving things can produce something that is living. But Dr. Pasteur used his scientific knowledge to show that this does not happen. People who believe in evolution have to believe in spontaneous generation because they do not believe in God. They were very upset when Pasteur proved that living things can come only from other living things, because that showed evolution could not be true.

Dr. Pasteur was a man who firmly believed in God, and who was not afraid to let others know of his belief, especially as he grew older. The more marvelous his discoveries, the more humble he became, because he knew that he was studying the things God created in nature. When people asked him about his faith, he told them that the more he learned from science, the stronger his faith in God became. An atheist of our generation,

Dr. Pasteur used his scientific knowledge to show that "spontaneous generation" does not happen.

who also was a scientist, called Pasteur "one of the greatest scientists in history." Indeed, he was a great scientist, with a great belief in God. We need more boys and girls, and men and women, who, like Dr. Pasteur, are not ashamed to stand up for God!

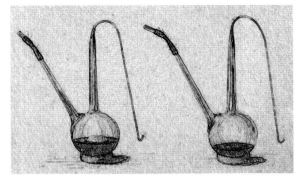
Drawing of one of Louis Pasteur's experiments

GEORGE WASHINGTON CARVER (1864-1943)

One of the most interesting scientists who believed in God was a man named George Washington Carver. He was born to parents who were slaves. When he was ten, he decided to educate himself. By the time he was 32, he had a Masters degree. Carver became the director of agricultural research at the Tuskegee Institute in Alabama. There he created and invented all sorts of amazing things. For example, Carver learned how to make 118 different products using a sweet potato. He developed over 300 products using the peanut. Once, he invited several friends for dinner. He served them all sorts of good things to eat like salad, soup, a creamed "vegetable," "chicken," coffee, cookies, and ice cream. His friends did not know, however, that all the items he served were made out of peanuts.

George Washington Carver was an amazing inventor. But he also believed strongly in God. He would go for long walks in the mornings and think about God. On Sunday afternoons, he taught Bible class at Tuskegee where he would read from the Scriptures. He once said that he studied the peanut so that he could find out why God had made it. He was very smart, and he believed in God.

SIR ISAAC NEWTON
(1642-1727)

One encyclopedia said that Sir Isaac Newton was "one of the greatest names in the history of human thought." Albert Einstein, one of the most popular scientists ever to have lived, said that his work would have been impossible without the work done by Newton. When Newton was in his twenties, he was recognized as a genius in science. He invented the mathematical computation known as calculus. He was the first person to seriously study the laws of gravity and explain how gravity can hold planets in place. Sir Isaac did much research on light and vision, and also invented the reflecting telescope. Newton once said: "... God is a living, intelligent, and powerful Being.... He is supreme, and most perfect." Newton was a genius scientist who believed that the Universe had a Designer and Creator.

OTHER MEN OF SCIENCE

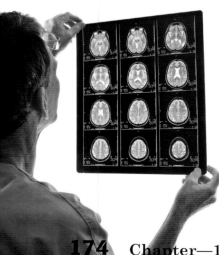

Many other scientists in the past also believed in God. Men like Johannes Kepler, the German astronomer, Michael Faraday, the British chemist, and Galileo Galilei, an Italian astronomer, all believed in a supernatural Creator. Carolus Linnaeus, who is recognized as the greatest taxonomist in the history of the world, was a believer in God. Also, there are many scientists in modern times who believe in God. Raymond Damadian invented the medical procedure known as MRI (magnetic resonance imaging). A.E. Wilder-Smith held three earned doctorates from three European universities. Melvin A. Cook won the 1968 E.G. Murphee Award in Industrial and Engineering Chemistry from the American Chemical Society. And Dmitri Kouznetsov, M.D, Ph.D., D.Sc., won the Komsomol Lenin Prize in 1983, distinguishing himself as one of the two most promising scientists in Russia at the time.

We should not believe in creation just because these brilliant scientists believed in creation. In fact, we should look at the evidence and decide for ourselves. On the other hand, we should never let those who believe in evolution get away with saying that all the smart people believe in evolution. That simply is not true. Thousands of intelligent men and women all over the world believe that God created this Universe, and that the Bible is His Word. The evidence that we see in the Universe proves that this is true. As Scottish physicist Sir David Brewster once asked, "What can the highest intellect on Earth do but bow to God's Word?"

||||||||||||||||||||||||||||||||||||||||||||||||||||||||||||||||||||||||||||

"What can the highest intellect on Earth do but bow to God's Word?"

Scottish physicist
Sir David Brewster

||||||||||||||||||||||||||||||||||||||||||||||||||||||||||||||||||||||||||||

CHAPTER REVIEW

FILL IN THE BLANKS

1. There are thousands of brilliant men and women who believe in _____.

2. When _____ was in his twenties, he was recognized as a genius in science.

3. We should not believe in creation just because many brilliant _____ believe in creation.

4. One of the world's top _____ scientists (who believed in God) was a man by the name of Wernher von Braun.

5. George Washington Carver developed 300 products using the _____.

SHORT ANSWER

1. Is it true to say that all the smart people believe in evolution? Why or why not?

2. Even though many intelligent people believe in creation, does that prove that it is true? Explain your answer.

3. Why is truth never based on majority vote or the logical fallacy known as the "bandwagon" argument?

4. Discuss why you think many intelligent people in the past and present believe in creation.

5. What are some of the reasons that creation scientists themselves give for their belief in God?

MULTIPLE CHOICE

1. George Washington Carver made about 118 products with this
   A. Peanut
   B. Sweet potato
   C. Spinach
   D. Brussel sprouts

2. He was a very influential space scientist
   A. George Washington Carver
   B. Isaac Newton
   C. Wernher von Braun
   D. Raymond Damadian

3. He invented the MRI
   A. George Washington Carver
   B. Isaac Newton
   C. Wernher von Braun
   D. Raymond Damadian

4. The letters MRI stand for
   A. Magnetic resonance imaging
   B. Motorized reel indicator
   C. Mom's rule intensifier
   D. None of the above

5. A form of his name appears on many modern dairy products
   A. George Washington Carver
   B. Louis Pasteur
   C. Wernher von Braun
   D. Raymond Damadian

6. A famous Scottish physicist who believed in God
   A. George Washington Carver
   B. Isaac Newton
   C. Wernher von Braun
   D. David Brewster

INDEX

N

O

P

R

S

CREDITS